GROW YOUR BUSINESS
WITHOUT
GROWING APART

A NEW PARADIGM FOR
ENTREPRENEURIAL COUPLES

BY

KELLY CLEMENTS

GROW YOUR BUSINESS WITHOUT GROWING APART
A new paradigm for entrepreneurial couples

Copyright © 2023 by Kelly Clements

To request permissions, contact the publisher at publish@joapublishing.com or Kelly@theentreprenewer.com

Hardback ISBN: 978-1-961098-04-6
Paperback ISBN: 978-1-961098-02-2
E-book ISBN: 978-1-961098-03-9
Printed in the USA.

Joan of Arc Publishing
Meridian, ID 83646
www.joapublishing.com

BONUS TOOLS

Click the QR code to get immediate
access to these powerful tools:

Power of Play

Power of Praise

Power of Purpose

Power of Provision

Power of Protection

Power of Pursuit

**This QR code is found throughout the book
and gives you access to all resources.**

PRAISE FOR KELLY CLEMENTS

"My husband (an entrepreneur) and I have worked with Kelly 3 different times over the last 4 years. She has been more than helpful (that's why I keep going back). She can quickly discern obstacles and challenges and help navigate a path for success. We love Kelly!"

—Robyn B.

****

"Kelly has been my relationship coach for about a year. She's amazing. All I can say is that last spring, I was on the verge of leaving. Kelly helped me get my relationship back to an amazing place.

Then, some new challenges have come up the last 2 months and she's now working with us as a couple, helping both of us and I'm constantly surprised how quick the changes are coming for us. She gets to the root of our problems quickly and accurately.

I trust her 100% to help lead you through your current challenges."

—Julia L.

****

"The work that I have done with Kelly as my coach has been nothing short of transformational. My relationship with my family, my success at my company, my health and wellness, my finances, my friendships, my fun—all have been positively affected. I highly recommend working with her!"

—Dave S.

*****

"I was looking for a coach for well over a year and I didn't find anyone that was the right fit. Too many are either more like a shrink or straight executive coach. Kelly's genius for growing a business and a relationship are a rare find!"

—Kyle B.

*****

"Great work! This teaching confirms how blessed I am with the most wonderful soulmate God created just for me. Thanks, Kelly!"

*****

This book is dedicated

to all who are brave enough

to do this work.

Keep Going.

TABLE OF CONTENTS

INTRODUCTION

I know that trying to figure out how to fix your relationship while growing a business is overwhelming. You're more confident in the business landscape; at least there you have KPIs, metrics, and a general sense of what works and what doesn't.

I know you bear incredible responsibility, make hundreds of decisions each day, and surf the tidal wave of emotions from excitement and possibility to fear and uncertainty. You can't turn your mind off and you're either at work or thinking about work. You may even think that *that's* the problem.

I know you want a healthy, expansive, and inspiring connection with your partner, but you may not know how to get there. You may have even found that traditional approaches like couples therapy or date nights didn't quite make the impact you were hoping for.

I also know, beyond the shadow of a doubt, that getting your relationship on track, aligning with your partner, and running life as if it's a three-legged race become the fuel that will catapult you to the next level in love *and* business.

1

Entrepreneurs are a unique breed and require different relationship strategies to offset the demands of owning a business. Spouses or partners of entrepreneurs experience their own unique journey that few on the outside understand.

This book will present those strategies for both the entrepreneur and the spouse. You'll learn the unique Alpha-Omega Framework developed exclusively for entrepreneurs to help balance the scales in your relationship. You'll also learn the six Presence Principles that will give you a dashboard to relationship success.

You'll learn how to save your marriage without saying a word. This won't require difficult conversations, awkward silences, or downward spirals of rehashing the past. We're going to pull you out of any nosedive you may be in by giving you a brand new outlook on your entrepreneurial relationship.

So grab a pen, a highlighter, and a notebook and settle in. You've got this, and I'm behind you all the way.

HOW TO MAXIMIZE THIS BOOK

While the advantages and complexities of entrepreneurial relationships are consistent, every relationship offers its own set of nuances. We need to address those nuances so the content works for you and your partner.

To begin, I define an entrepreneurial couple as a **romantic couple where at least one of you is an entrepreneur**.

The combinations of entrepreneurial couples could include any of the following:

- two entrepreneurs in the same business

- two entrepreneurs in separate businesses

- an entrepreneur with a spouse who holds more traditional employment

- an entrepreneur with a spouse who doesn't work outside the home

As long as one of you is an entrepreneur, I'm confident you'll find this content to be relevant and relatable.

However, there are a few relationship variables that may require you to hold roles and pronouns loosely as you read this book.

I am going to speak through the very general lens that the man is the entrepreneur and the woman is the spouse. This is NOT because I have a judgment that that's how it should be. It's just easier. For two years I fumbled with all the combinations of pronouns and roles, and it created too much complexity for the reader.

So, if you fall in one of the three variable categories below, simply change the roles or pronouns so they reflect your relationship.

Those variables include the following

- being in a committed, long-term relationship but not married

- same sex couples

- "role-reversed" relationships (where the woman is the entrepreneur)

ALL entrepreneurial couples will benefit from this message and all are celebrated in expanding in marriage and business by adjusting the roles and pronouns to reflect your unique relationship.

When gender matters above role (entrepreneur or spouse), I will make a point to call that out.

Simply look for the $\Omega\Omega\Omega\Omega$ box. This will provide expanded insight on how gender dynamics impact that particular topic.

There's one other important factor to consider. These strategies have already helped thousands of entrepreneurial couples create the love relationship of their dreams. So . . .

If you're part of the small minority looking for validation that your relationship is on the right track, this book will work for you.

4

If you're part of the larger majority looking for inspiration to help make an ordinary relationship extraordinary, this book will work for you.

If you're part of the sweet spot of my heart, here in desperation, looking for a Hail Mary to save a relationship that's hanging on by a thread, this book *might* work for you. It might be the missing link that helps you turn your relationship around and sends you off into the sunset together. I hope it does.

Or, it may be the permission slip you need to leave. If you and your partner are just inherently toxic together, these strategies will not work for you. I've found that there's an equally powerful gift in that awareness, though. I do not believe in teaching people how to cope with toxic relationships—the collateral damage is too great for everyone involved.

In short, it takes two happy, healthy people to create a happy, healthy relationship. I encourage you to use this book to ensure you're doing your part to show up as a happy, healthy individual. It will pay off in your marriage, your business, and every other aspect of life.

This is also going to require both of you to have a growth mindset. This is accomplished by challenging your existing beliefs about yourself, your partner, and relationships in general.

And if you really want to nail this, we need to start with something as basic as your coachability. I'm going to invite both of you to take a posture of curiosity, openness, recognition, complete ownership, and positive expectancy.

MEET YOUR GUIDE . . .

I first noticed the positive impact a healthy relationship had on entrepreneurs way back in 2004. I had just started working as a program advisor for an entrepreneurial coaching company called Strategic Coach.

If you're not familiar, "Strategic Coach® is a Business Coaching Program For Growth-Minded Entrepreneurs. Strategic Coach® is an organization run by entrepreneurs for entrepreneurs—the recognized leader worldwide in entrepreneurial coaching. For over 30 years, they've worked with more than 20,000 successful business owners from around the globe to help them achieve faster growth, greater profits, and an exceptional quality of life."

So, at the age of twenty-five, I got to spend my workdays in workshop rooms filled with successful entrepreneurs. They were there to learn how to "work less and make more." It was my role to help them integrate what they learned in their workshops into their businesses back home.

Can you imagine all of the lessons I learned behind those doors?

I learned about lucrative deals and ludicrous lawsuits. I helped my clients build dream teams and fire nightmare clients. I coached them on increasing confidence and reducing complexity. I watched my clients turn crazy ideas into industry transformers. I walked with them through cash crunches, hypergrowth, marriage, and divorce... I heard the highs and lows and loved it all.

But there was one thing that was glaringly obvious to me.

My clients who raved about their spouses or partners as their top supporters were hitting higher levels of success with less stress and more fulfillment than their unhappily married or single counterparts. These happily partnered clients achieved great success even if their supportive spouse or partner never set foot in the business.

There was just some sort of . . . ease that these clients had on their path to success. They went further, faster. The best example I can use to illustrate this is the Clydesdale. This working draft horse can pull 8,000 pounds on its own. It would stand to reason, then, that adding another horse would double its pulling capacity to 16,000 pounds. However, that's inaccurate. Two Clydesdales, when working together, can TRIPLE their individual pulling capacity to 24,000 pounds! It's the ultimate 1+1= 3 synergy that I had been observing in my clients with thriving love relationships.

It would take me a few years and one helluva journey to understand why, but what I discovered I will share with you here.

This was a deeply personal lesson that led to a massive transformation, not only for me, but for all of my clients, and now, hopefully for you.

You see, when I was working at Strategic Coach, I was a newlywed: a fresh, starry-eyed, twenty-five-year-old woman who was just beginning her career and her marriage. I had finally "settled down" after a prolonged season of traveling the world after college and I was ready to make the most out of adult life. As I sat in those workshop rooms, listening to all of these stories, I fell head-over-heels in love with entrepreneurship.

I admired the impact entrepreneurship had on local communities and the world. I envied the freedom that working for yourself offered. I was impressed by the financial risks and rewards the entrepreneurial journey offered. I wanted all of that and more for my husband and myself.

I came home from work every day, excited to share with my husband what I had learned that day. Pretty soon, my stories turned into suggestions and ultimately requests for us to start a business together. He humored me at first, but as the months and years went by he grew weary. One day, he finally blurted out *"Why can't this just be enough for you? Why do you always need more?!"*

If you've ever tried to make an entrepreneur out of a "not-a-preneur," you know the frustration this brings to both people.

This would begin our drift to what I now call The Ambition Gap.

We had started out as equals and had a great balance of shared experiences and individual interests, but over time, that changed. My interests grew and my priorities evolved. My worldview was changing and I became more interested in my personal growth.

Eventually, the only thing we had in common was an address and the two most adorable boys in the world: Will and Luke. At the time of this writing, Will is fifteen and Luke is thirteen. They are both great students, stellar athletes, total gentlemen, and budding entrepreneurs. Will has the most peaceful, calming presence blended with an effortless imagination that simultaneously grounds me and inspires me. Luke has a capacity for love and communication that blows my ever-loving mind. Thinking about either of them can instantly put a lump in my throat and a tear in my eye.

But because I didn't know then what I know now, I've spent half my nights, half my weekends, and half my holidays without them. So when I tell you this is personal, it's as personal as it gets.

You see, when I was married to their dad, I was the Alpha.

> Alpha, if you're not familiar, is the more dominant partner. Alpha's are self-assured, self-preserving leaders who are confident, driven, and unyielding. Alphas are wired for maintaining their independence. They know their safety, security, and autonomy is essential for their personal advancement, and thereby, their tribe's advancement.

I was so consumed with bigger, better, faster, stronger, I missed the fact that my ambition wasn't inspiring him; it was stunting him.

My stories became comparisons and my suggestions became criticisms. I started judging his contentment as laziness and forced him into a box of incompetence with my constant complaints. My expectations of him got lower and lower and every single time, he was proving me right. He was feeling constantly criticized and I was feeling chronically disappointed.

My prize for winning every argument was a complete shell of a partner. Play stupid games, win stupid prizes.

He'd go on to win an actual prize. About one year after we divorced, he called and asked if I could keep the kids for an extra week. "Yeah, of course!" I exclaimed, excited for the extra time with them.

"Thanks. I won the President's Award at work. I'm in the top 1% of sales. I'll be in Hawaii for ten days with my new girlfriend."

"Wait? What!! I couldn't get him out of bed before noon!" I thought. "And *now* he's crushing it?"

It turns out his new girlfriend was an elementary school teacher and thought he put the stars in the sky—and so he did.

I had a flashback to all those clients raving about how they owed all their business success to their supportive spouse. This was one of the first of many lessons I learned: you have to BE a supportive partner to HAVE a supportive partner.

Can you relate to being in a relationship where "leadership" gets taken too far? Unfortunately, karma caught up with me really quickly when, in my next relationship, I discovered what life was like with a fellow Alpha. That story is continued at the end of Chapter 2: Understanding Alpha.

Both of these relationships, coupled with my professional coaching background, have uniquely positioned me to support entrepreneurs and their spouses in growing their businesses while deepening their marriages.

If this sounds like a dynamic you'd like resolved in your relationship, but you haven't figured out how to solve it, this is exactly what The Alpha-Omega Framework in Part One will address. I'm going to show you how to bridge The Ambition Gap to create marital harmony.

I designed the The Alpha-Omega Framework exclusively for entrepreneurs and their partners and I'm confident both of you will find liberation, balance, and deeper connection through this perspective.

The foundation of The Alpha-Omega Framework is The Relationship Spectrum.

PART I

UNDERSTANDING
THE RELATIONSHIP SPECTRUM

Power dynamics are one reason entrepreneurial relationships are so challenging. As natural leaders, entrepreneurs can struggle with how the traits that make them successful in business can be challenging in personal relationships.

For example, if you're driven in business, you may be a control freak at home. If you're creative in business, you might be chaos at home. Great delegator in business? Lazy at home. You get the gist.

The same is true for the partner. If partners are supportive, they may lack personal ambition. If they're content, entrepreneurs may see them as lazy.

Ironically, it's often the same traits that we're initially attracted to that end up being the biggest pain points later on in the relationship.

Because all of our strengths and weaknesses are Buy One, Get One, I'll never suggest changing these traits. But I am going to show you how to identify when those traits are working *for* you, and when they're working *against* you.

We'll do this by understanding The Relationship Spectrum. The Relationship Spectrum consists of two conjoined spectrums: The Alpha Spectrum and The Beta Spectrum. It looks like this:

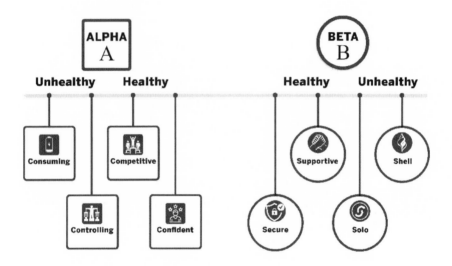

One of you will fall on The Alpha Spectrum, and one of you will fall on The Beta Spectrum. The first step is to determine who is Alpha, and who is Beta. Generally speaking, the entrepreneur falls on The Alpha Spectrum and their spouse is on The Beta Spectrum. However, I know plenty of couples who insist it's actually the other way around. We'll spend the next couple chapters learning about both spectrums. You'll have a better understanding of which partner is which by the end of Part One.

Right now, I'd just like you to get a feel for the full spectrum. And, spoiler alert, if you feel like you're being swallowed up by The Ambition Gap, it's probably because one or both of you is on the Unhealthy end of your respective spectrum.

The goal for both of you will be to shift back into healthy territory. When both people are in healthy territory, it creates the perfect spark that reignites that intimate chemistry we're after.

Chapter 1

UNDERSTANDING ALPHA

If you're an entrepreneur, chances are pretty high that you're also the Alpha in your personal life. Again, Alpha is the more dominant partner—the leader. They are self-assured, confident, driven, and unyielding. Alphas are wired for self-preservation and maintaining their independence. They know their personal security and autonomy is essential for their personal advancement, and thereby, their tribe's advancement.

Alphas love a good challenge and have a knack for enrolling others into their endeavors. They resist being controlled by others. The fear of someone else determining their circumstances drives them to maintain their independence at all costs.

If you're the Alpha, the good news is that you're already wired for self-preservation and growth. This chapter will show you how to maximize those superpowers.

The bad news is that when presented with potentially confronting information, Alphas can shut down, take a "go f*ck yourself" approach, and miss an opportunity for growth.

If you feel like you get triggered with this framework, remember to keep a growth mindset. Let that trigger be your indicator that you're on the verge of a massive breakthrough. Embracing growth in this area will radically upgrade your relationship, your business, and your life.

The Alpha Spectrum runs from Confident Alpha (Healthy) to Consuming Alpha (Unhealthy). By the end of this chapter, you will be able to identify where you fall on The Alpha Spectrum. You will also be able to navigate your way to the highest ranks of Alpha: Confident Alpha.

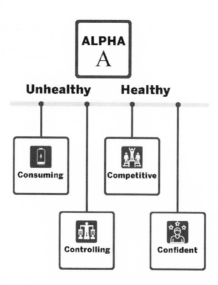

HEALTHY ALPHA

We start with Healthy Alpha because we begin with the end in mind. I want you to have the vision of what Healthy Alpha looks like so it's easier for you to break any bad habits of Unhealthy Alpha you may possess.

Achieving Healthy Alpha is the pinnacle of leadership. Here, you create and lead with confidence and security. You have a trusted team that helps you multiply your already remarkable gifts. Healthy Alphas have experienced the benefit of trusted teamwork and recognize extraordinary results require extraordinary relationships.

Healthy Alphas have an innate understanding of the oxygen-mask theory: that by taking care of themselves first, they are better equipped to care for everyone around them.

Moreover, Healthy Alpha offers relief from the constant vigilance and rage experienced by Unhealthy Alpha. Healthy Alphas understand that not everyone is out to get them and don't waste unnecessary energy protecting themselves from irrelevant threats.

There are two types of Alpha on the Healthy side of the spectrum: Confident Alpha and Competitive Alpha.

Confident Alpha

The ultimate leader of the pack, Confident Alphas' attributes include grounded confidence blended with genuine curiosity or interest. They are respectful, balanced, poised, and forthcoming. They don't skirt around issues or shy away from difficult conversations. They have many tools for conflict resolution and understand that preserving the relationship with dignity and respect is more important than winning an argument.

Confident Alphas are congruent across all areas of life. Their families feel as respected and protected as the business. Their team members feel supported and empowered.

They feel responsible for the needs and desires of others and will factor that into decision making. They are respected by their friends and family and operate without ulterior motives. They use their vision and gifts to create a better life for everyone around them.

Confident Alphas have conquered one of the greatest fears among Alphas: letting others in. They have experienced the power of an open heart and discovered how much energy it frees up from the emotional armor they had learned to bear.

Confident Alphas have released their anger toward anyone who has wronged them. They recognize that all of life's setbacks have happened *for* them (not *to* them), making them a better, more compassionate leader.

While they have little tolerance for jackassery, they are willing to recognize imperfections in themselves and others.

Competitive Alpha

As we move further along The Alpha Spectrum, competition starts to appear. While competition in the marketplace fuels an Alpha, competition in the love relationship is more complex. When it comes to your relationship, healthy competition doesn't *interfere* with your connection to your partner—it *fosters* it. Competitive Alphas take on challenges, not to prove their independence but to stretch themselves and those around them to become even better.

Did you know that the origin of competition was not a contest used to decide winners and losers or to determine who was better or worse than another? It was actually used as a tool of collaboration by which both participants were able to apply their gifts and talents in real time, allowing both to grow and expand simultaneously. The result of competition in its truest spirit is that both come out as winners— not because "everyone gets a trophy," but because both have expanded through the same shared experience.

This is the spirit of competition that Competitive Alphas have mastered in their personal relationships. They don't win at the cost of their partner; they win to the benefit of their partner. They carry their partner with them when they win, knowing both are growing and expanding through their loving collaboration. And when their partner wins, they celebrate their partner as their most worthy mate, helping to lead the way to shared expansion.

Competitive Alphas enjoy a heightened sense of aliveness as they work to find the edge of who they can trust and who poses an actual threat. They may require strong evidence that their partner is safe before they let their guard down. When they do get the opportunity to let that guard down, they are able to connect with their partner in a powerfully intimate way, offering relief and inspiration to both people.

When the competition is friendly and motivates both people to become better, the competition is useful. However, there is a tipping point with competition. If taken too seriously, someone has to win and someone has to lose. This begins to fray the true teamwork dynamic necessary for a relationship to thrive.

Competitive Alpha stays on the healthy end of the spectrum as long as they feel secure with their own personal confidence, resources, and success. However, in times of scarcity or insecurity, they may dip into Unhealthy Alpha, throwing walls back up and becoming more shrewd.

If you feel your partnership is slipping toward being competitive *against* one another, attention is required. Remind yourself that your partner is, in fact, your partner—not a competitor to overcome. If you don't correct this competitive posture now, you're at risk of slipping into the Unhealthy side of The Alpha Spectrum.

UNHEALTHY ALPHA

I've found that, occasionally, there can be a slow fade from Healthy to Unhealthy. A person who starts out as a Healthy Alpha can slide into Unhealthy territory over time or when unexpected stressors arise. Or, as couples get more comfortable with one another, the Healthy Alpha facade begins to crumble. It is nearly impossible for Unhealthy Alpha to have a fulfilling relationship with anybody, so even if you're Healthy Alpha, skim this part; you'll want to know what to avoid.

When your spouse confronts you, do you come back twice as hard or shut down completely? Does your partner feel like the punishment doesn't fit the crime? Are you well aware that you can use your anger to "keep others in line"? If so, you're probably an Unhealthy Alpha.

This is when *relationships* start to feel like *situationships*. True connection, intimacy, and partnership are replaced by control, distance, and judgment.

The Unhealthy side of the spectrum is where "leadership" (control) begins to erode connection. It's not just leadership that gets taken too far. It's when all of those magnificent traits that successful entrepreneurs possess get taken too far.

It's not uncommon for partners of Unhealthy Alpha to describe their partner completely differently than they are perceived in public. Take a look at the comparison below:

If in business you are . . .	At home you may be . . .
Passionate	Emotional
Ambitious	Never Satisfied
Driven	A Workaholic
Innovative	Out of touch
Creative	Manic
Well-connected	Spread too thin
Holding a Standard of Excellence	A Perfectionist/Overly Critical
Quick	Reckless/Unrealistic
Growth-oriented	Selfish

The best way I can describe this is that bright lights cast stark shadows. No one knows your shadow side better than your spouse. But they've stuck with you this far, and I'd venture a bet that says they love you in spite of your shadow.

Most spouses of Unhealthy Alphas appreciate the talents and recognize the accomplishments of their partner. But more than anything, they live in fear of upsetting Unhealthy Alpha.

They cling to the knowingness that with therapy or coaching, their partner could round out their rough edges and rise to Healthy Alpha. They may recognize that Unhealthy Alpha lashes out from a deep-seated fear or insecurity. They may even (falsely) believe that if they get really skilled at keeping Unhealthy Alpha happy, life would finally be as good as it looks from the outside. We'll talk about this more in the next Chapter, Understanding Beta.

There are two types of Alpha on the Unhealthy side of the spectrum: Controlling Alpha and Consuming Alpha.

Controlling Alpha

You can *connect* with your partner or you can *control* them, but you cannot do both.

Controlling Alphas are hyper concerned with what their partner is doing. They use ultimatums and worst-case scenarios in an attempt to influence their partner's choices. They may feel they are protecting their partner and the relationship, but their partner experiences it as control.

Keep in mind, "protection" is often a noble way of saying "control." You'll know if you are being protective or controlling based on your intentions. Are you or your partner actually in danger? Or do you fear losing control over a situation? **Your fear of losing control is your growth opportunity, not your partner's responsibility.**

Controlling Alpha has limited interest in their partner's needs and desires. They become shut down and crabby when things don't go their way. Silence and anger become the punishment for veering off of Controlling Alpha's agenda.

Controlling Alphas have limited resources when it comes to conflict management. When the only tool you have is a hammer, everything becomes a nail. This presents as tyrannical "leadership" and is often driven by insecurity.

However, in times of extreme confidence, safety, and security, there may be glimpses of a lovable leader. These moments, while they may be fleeting and sporadic, keep a spouse holding on for brighter days.

Consuming Alpha

On the most extreme end of Unhealthy Alpha is Consuming Alpha. Named for the way they leave their partner feeling, Consuming Alphas disregard personal boundaries and aim to govern all aspects of life. They cast judgment on every area of their partner's life as a way to force submission.

Consuming Alphas push a fixed narrative that there is nothing wrong with them, accusing everyone else of being the problem. Their argument can be so persuasive that even their partner begins to believe it.

Consuming Alphas have extreme reactions to even the slightest disruptions. For instance, if their partner takes longer than expected to have lunch with a friend, Consuming Alpha might withhold resources including attention, affection, or finances. This is a tactic used to keep their partners in line and may also be referred to as grooming.

Consuming Alphas have an inability to stay emotionally connected. They feel a sense of urgency to keep their guard up at all times. They may churn through friends, team members, and even lovers because they take others for granted, refusing to let anyone in. They believe relationships are disposable and can cast others aside over a disagreement. They often feel betrayed over differences of opinions and hold grudges for unreasonable amounts of time. They may even hold the belief that they are doing all this to toughen-up everyone around them.

With a Consuming Alpha, everything is a strategy. They are constantly scanning their environment and strategizing ways to manipulate people and circumstances to ensure they come out on top. Similarly, their partners are constantly strategizing ways to communicate or engage with them depending on Consuming Alpha's mood.

Paradoxically, because they have worked so hard to ensure they aren't rejected by others, they end up fast-tracking that rejection. They consume others with their impossible demands and egregious opinions, reducing their partner to a shell of a human.

Gotta say it: in extreme cases of Unhealthy Alpha, abuse may be present. Here is an additional resource for you:

Not to People Like Us: The Hidden Abuse in Upscale Marriages by Susan Weitzman

---

ΩΩΩΩ

If you are a woman in the Unhealthy Alpha zone, your biggest priority is to work on your relationship with your own feminine energy. Understand that as a woman, your words either breathe life into your man, or suck the life out of him. Ensuring that your words are affirming and encouraging will help empower your man to powerfully rise as your equal. There are many other strengths that become available to you through your feminine energy, but affirming language will have the quickest positive impact on your relationship.

UNHEALTHY ALPHA RECOVERY PLAN

Dan Sullivan, founder of Strategic Coach, says, "All progress starts by telling the truth." So if you've identified as Unhealthy Alpha and you're still reading, you've already accomplished the hardest part— acknowledging a growth opportunity.

As an Alpha, you're willing to take on extraordinary challenges. Whether it's starting a new enterprise, competing in extreme competitions like an Iron-Man, taking ice baths, walking on hot coals, detoxing your liver, building muscle, or expanding your mind, you're always up for conquering new territory. But how bold are you when it comes to opening your heart?

What if you recognized that the walls you throw up to keep others out are actually your prison of loneliness and self-deception?

The Victim, The Villain, and The Victor

The journey from Unhealthy Alpha to Healthy Alpha requires an inner deep dive that journeys from Victim to Villain in order to become the Victor.

Unhealthy Alpha is, ironically, in victim mode. He likely feels disconnected from his spouse because she isn't keeping up. He may feel like she's let herself go or that she's the only person in his life who doesn't admire and respect him. He likely has scores of evidence that he's respectable; he's committed to growth and expansion, but she has come to feel like dead weight. He feels like their marriage has become a bigger burden than a blessing and begins to track all the ways she's holding him back. He may even say things like, "Screw her. She's not that special. I can find someone else to do my laundry."

In order to shift toward Healthy Alpha, he must recognize his contribution to the unraveling of the relationship. This requires confronting his inner Villain.

It's recognizing his critical comments or his comparisons of his spouse to others. It may be admitting that in his insistence that she should be more goal-oriented, he disregarded her needs, gifts, and sacrifice. He may need to own that he prioritized work over home because work provided an effortless fan base, where home required more presence and a deep dive on becoming emotionally available.

Even more confronting is taking total ownership of the bulldozing, undermining, gaslighting, stonewalling, punishing, cheating, withholding, controlling, sedating, escaping, avoiding, shaming, and blaming. Only when he recognizes these behaviors is he able to identify healthier leadership practices going forward.

He will become the Victor as Healthy Alpha when instead of demanding, he requests. Instead of blaming, he inquires. Instead of bulldozing, controlling, shaming, and blaming, he invites. Gaslighting and stonewalling give way to accepting total responsibility.

That Jagged Edge

Unhealthy Alphas often believe the ax they're grinding—that jagged edge—is what drives their success. They dare not tamper with that edge for fear that it's like the crucial Jenga® piece, and that pulling that block would collapse their ivory tower.

Unfortunately, this is another scenario where what (you believe) drives success in business causes challenges at home. When I work with Unhealthy Alphas, I tell them they can keep the edge. Keep the mask, keep the sword, keep as much armor as you'd like.

But can I ask you just to consider your next heroic act to be *letting your partner in*? Are you willing to consider the best-case scenario of what life would be like if you just put the sword down at home? Are you willing to see just how damn good you could be if instead of protecting yourself from your partner, you aligned with her? What's possible if you stop squaring off against your partner, and start running life with her?

Damned if She Does, Damned if She Doesn't

As an Unhealthy Alpha, you are likely the bottleneck to everything you desire in your life and relationship. You may try to delegate projects to those around you, but never fully get everything off your plate. You probably find that tasks are never done to your standards or everyone is waiting on your directive to drive completion. When I work with spouses of entrepreneurs, what I often hear is, "He's impossible to please. He gets upset when the credit card bill is too high, but then gets mad when I don't book us in first class." This damned-if-you-do, damned-if-you-don't scenario paralyzes the partner, leaving the entrepreneur constantly feeling let down.

You have extraordinary gifts and capacity for success, yet diminish it with the resistance you cast in your relationships. No matter how hard you work, you will only ever be working at 33% capacity because you've thwarted that 1+1= 3 synergy I explained in the Introduction with the Clydesdale example. How much more could you produce if you didn't exert so much extra energy judging every decision your spouse makes?

Your judgment of your partner (or anyone for that matter) for *not being enough* (capable enough, smart enough, clean enough, efficient enough) puts her in a defensive posture, guided by fear and survivalism. As humans, we can either create or defend. If your partner is so busy defending herself (even if it's silently in her head), she won't be in a position to help create with you. She's paralyzed trying to figure out which land mine to avoid.

Understanding Judgment

Here's a hard but necessary truth for your recovery. Judgment is a reflection of shame.

Your judgment of other people is part of the sword you use to keep others away from your own shame closet. I know shame is a squirmy word, but if we're going to do the work, we can't *not* talk about it.

There are two things I want you to know about shame:

1) *Sometimes* it starts as bliss. We start doing something that we know to be wrong; call it drinking, drugs, gambling, an affair, shopping, porn, or even work. The temporary relief it offers is really a form of connection. It's filling a void, and for a moment, it offers BLISS *because* it offers

CONNECTION. (Please visit geniusrecovery.org for more context and cutting edge resources about addiction.) In recognizing this, I'd like you to consider if opening your heart to your partner would allow you to feel an authentic, genuine connection, and if that connection would offer you greater, sustainable BLISS without the hangover of shame. Which brings me to my second point:

2) Shame grows and thrives in secrecy. Like cockroaches in the dark, when we lock it away, it spreads to every corner of our being. Somehow the shame seems to grow, making us feel more and more unlovable. Sometimes, we lock it away so deep, we can barely recognize or remember it ourselves. We take out the sword and start slashing every time we sense someone is getting close to that shame closet. However, the second we shine the light on it by way of sharing our stories, just like those cockroaches, they scatter, seemingly disappearing. This doesn't mean you need to go on a big PR campaign and confess all your misgivings to everyone you've ever known. It does mean that sharing your journey with your partner, letting her into that vault, may turn that shame closet into a portal of intimacy and connection that would blow your world wide open in the best possible way.

This is the transformational power of an open heart. It metabolizes the head trash that shame produces and converts it into the nectar of love and connection. It takes the very thing you *think* makes you unlovable and transmutes it into an unbreakable bond. But the heart needs to be OPEN and unguarded to function at this capacity.

The Game Plan

I invite you to consider how life might open up for you if you addressed your Unhealthy Alpha. I'm not going to ask you to change. Maintaining your Alpha posture isn't up for discussion. But can you shift? Can you move, one click at a time, toward Healthy Alpha?

Can you start to find positive evidence of what happens when you trust others? Can you lean into the relief of having a life where it doesn't feel like everyone's out to get you? Can you taste the freedom of not feeling responsible for punishing everyone around you?

What if you dropped the punitive reactions and created space for your partner to rise up out of creativity instead of shrinking out of fear? What if you recognized your relationship was a multiplier and that as your partner expands, everything in your life expands with her? What if you leaned into having a successful business *and* a healthy, thriving relationship?

In this space you activate your partner on a completely new level. You awaken her dormant power and in turn she welcomes you to even higher levels of expansion. Together, you create a vortex of upward growth and momentum that is so irresistible, you can feel the vibration of love in the mitochondria of your cells. Jesus, I want that for you, for humanity.

Can you make that move to Healthy Alpha, one small shift at a time?

Getting comfortable with your partner stepping forth in her full expression results in you enjoying a more balanced relationship full of chemistry, intimacy, and respect. Ironically, this requires **you** to be more confident and secure in yourself and your relationship. It's going to require you to start removing the walls around your heart.

Ways you can test yourself here are small but simple gestures. Here are a few you can try.

- A six-second hug. When you get home from work each day, go find your partner in the house. Pull her close to you and hold her for six seconds.

- Left-eye-to-left-eye eye contact. When you're speaking with her, hold direct eye contact with her left eye.

- Listen to her explain the best part of her day. Even if you can't relate to it, give her the space to share what's on her heart and experience her joy. If she can trust you with her joy, you'll get more of it.

- Implement The Presence Principles in Part Two of this book.

At the end of the day, it's Alpha's posture that determines how much space he creates for his partner. Unhealthy Alpha's end up forcing their partner away, or into Unhealthy Beta. But Healthy Alpha holds space and welcomes their partner's unique talents and gifts to expand the relationship.

***

Now, back to that story of karma when I went from Unhealthy Alpha in my marriage to Unhealthy Beta in my next relationship.

In that relationship, for the first time in my life, I experienced what it was like to be in my feminine. I discovered that feminine energy wasn't actually weak, but undeniably powerful. I experienced the relief of not having to make every decision. I learned the power of surrender and the delight of being led.

What was condemned in my marriage (always wanting more) was celebrated in this relationship. I was encouraged to dream bigger and challenged when I second guessed myself. I felt mutual respect as we saw and appreciated one another's gifts. We didn't have 1+1=3 synergy. We had 1+1=100 chemistry.

We effortlessly inspired one another to become better and push our limits. The chemistry was palpable and it truly felt like even the sky was too limiting for us.

Our fierce, independent spirits quickly blended into inter-dependence. But with no boundaries, and no clear vision of the future, we eventually faded into co-dependence.

In the early years, I was so intoxicated with his presence and our chemistry, I focused solely on what we were building, with no attention on what I was losing.

I was pouring everything I had into him and his business. I traded time with my friends to travel with him. When he got stressed, I lost sleep trying to figure out how to support him. When he needed help with something, I dropped everything I was doing to support him.

I was losing myself one tiny yet consistent decision at a time. The more I swooped in to help him, the more he depended on it. What once felt exhilarating began to feel exhausting. I had a ton of output going into the relationship, but I was feeling very little in return. The demands and stress of his business got the trump card on any situation or need I had.

When I felt stress or disappointment in my life, I was met with, "You have nothing to complain about. Your problems are a cakewalk compared to mine."

I stopped pursuing my own personal development because whatever I did never seemed to be good enough for him. He wanted me to grow- but not too much; and not in areas he didn't value. At some point, when new opportunities became available to me, it threatened him. Where I once felt solace in his arms, I later felt scared and on eggshells.

As the years passed, his stress and outbursts started to creep into every facet of life. Every decision I made had a land mine attached to it; it paralyzed me in my decision-making. What had once been a wide open, deep dive into the ocean of love and intimacy became a careful, piddly splash in the puddles. His fuse was getting shorter and it was getting harder and harder to tell what was going to set him off.

The irony of how I went from being the bulldozer in my marriage to the one getting steamrolled in this relationship was never lost on me. I had become a shell of my former self.

It all came to a head one day in my kitchen. We were arguing about the dwindling state of our relationship when he looked at me and asked, "Where's Kelly?! Where's the woman I fell in love with?

Where's the woman who could light up any room? Where'd she go?!"

I said something to the effect of, "Screw you! I've been on the floor waiting for the crumbs of your attention to fall! I'm not just a doll that you can take off the shelf every time you decide you want me to be available for you!"

At that moment, I realized he had not taken anything from me.

I had given it to him.

Instead of taking my "leadership" too far like I did in my marriage, I took my "support" too far in this relationship. I had betrayed myself in favor of the relationship. My support had become sacrifice at the expense of myself and, ultimately, my relationship. It was a slow fade, but sure enough, I had become Beta.

Chapter 2

UNDERSTANDING BETA

If Alpha is defined as the leader in the relationship, Beta is the follower. Beta is the more accommodating partner, the yielder. They can easily oblige, go with the flow, allow, and accept. They are wired to support and keep the peace, knowing their security is connected to the happiness of Alpha.

In a modern relationship, it is rare that the same person remains Beta through all domains of life. Modern couples share divided responsibility across different domains. This means that there are some areas of life where Alpha becomes Beta and vice versa. Use this as a guide for any and all areas where you may be the Beta.

In my experience, Beta is *usually* the spouse of the entrepreneur. However, there are plenty of couples who would say it's actually the entrepreneur who follows at home. Often, this is the result of learned or even forced helplessness. In this case, the entrepreneur likely has decision fatigue. Having made 600,000 decisions by the time he gets home, he has simply run out of capacity for critical thinking.

While this is completely understandable, it gives supporting evidence to the "business gets the best of you, I get the rest of you" narrative that many spouses feel.

And let's not underestimate the invisible workload that women carry that results in the same level of decision fatigue. If the entrepreneur takes a passive stance at home, he forces his wife into Alpha, which can automatically thwart romantic connection—more on this in Chapter 7: Provision (this shift alone will open up tremendous connectivity for you as a couple).

The goal of this chapter is to understand Beta. If you're Beta, you will gain a greater understanding of how to step more fully into yourself and your relationship. If your partner is Beta, you'll gain a broader perspective of what she might be experiencing in her relationship with you.

Like The Alpha Spectrum, The Beta Spectrum runs from Healthy Beta to Unhealthy Beta. By the end of this chapter, you will be able to identify where you fall on The Beta Spectrum. You will also be able to navigate your way toward the highest ranks of Beta: Secure Beta.

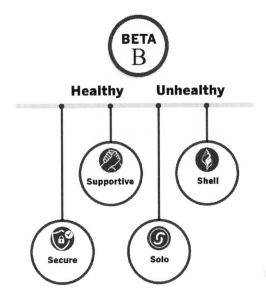

HEALTHY BETA

Again, we start with Healthy Beta because we begin with the end in mind. I want you to have the vision of what Healthy Beta looks like so it's easier for you to break any bad habits of Unhealthy Beta you may possess.

Maintaining Healthy Beta offers tremendous relief and fulfillment. Here, you are supportive and encouraging, yet maintain your own sense of self. You admire and respect your partner, but not at the expense of yourself. You embrace the power of allowing and receiving, but have maintained a fair degree of independence and self-reliance.

Healthy Betas also have an innate understanding of the oxygen-mask theory: that by taking care of themselves first, they are better equipped to care for everyone around them.

Healthy Betas have overcome the need to *earn* other people's love. Healthy Betas understand that each person is responsible for their own happiness and do not feel responsible for rescuing everyone around them.

There are two types of Beta on the Healthy side of the spectrum: Secure Beta and Supportive Beta.

Secure Beta

Secure Beta is supportive and engaged and able to take good care of themselves while supporting Alpha. They are in touch with the needs of others, but do not betray themselves to accommodate those needs.

Secure Betas feel loved without feeling like they need to earn love by people-pleasing. They are joyous, gracious, humble, and alive! They are open and expressive and love sharing their talents with others.

Secure Betas often reflect the best qualities of others right back to them, allowing their partner to experience the best in themselves.

They can see others as they are and embrace them with steadfast grace and acceptance.

Secure Betas understand their Alpha counterpart is up to big things in life, and they keep pace with them in the confidence that their support is a massive contribution to the advancement of the couple.

Secure Betas have overcome the need to earn others' love and recognize when it's time to let go of an unhealthy relationship. They have released their resentment of others who have let them down and know how to generate true fulfillment for themselves.

Secure Betas have maintained a strong sense of personal identity and don't get swayed by comparisons or expectations of others.

Supportive Beta

Adjacent to Secure Beta is Supportive Beta. Supportive Beta still has attention on Alpha, but is less likely *to prioritize* themselves. They are quick to fill their days supporting others, but have overcome their guilt in the occasional "indulgence" of self-care.

Supportive Betas don't only extend their charming, warm talents to their spouse; they extend it to everyone in their inner circle. Because the output of love and attention is so vast, they have also embraced the art of receiving. Supportive Betas have learned to allow others to return the favor and comfortably accept help from others when necessary.

Did you know one of the origins of the word *supportive* means "enable something to fulfill its function and remain in operation"? Supportive Betas take this role to heart and will give extraordinary attention to all of Alpha's needs. However, they may not recognize they have been abandoning their own needs until they reach burnout. Only then will they gladly take some time for themselves.

This dwindling act of self-care may start to disintegrate the personal fulfillment of Beta and therefore the health of the relationship. This is a tipping point. When personal fulfillment is diminished, it's difficult to stay connected to your partner, because you have begun to lose touch with yourself.

UNHEALTHY BETA

A person who starts out as a Healthy Beta can slide into unhealthy territory over time. I often hear, especially from women, that they have no idea how they became *so far gone* as they reminisce about a younger, more confident version of themselves. They recall the early times in the relationship, as responsibilities mounted, that they started prioritizing others above themselves. It's nearly impossible for Unhealthy Beta to have a satisfying relationship with anyone, so if you're Healthy Beta, keep skimming. You'll want to know what to avoid.

Are you feeling disconnected from your Self? Do you feel completely depleted from putting so much focus and energy on everyone else's needs? Do you wonder how you lost touch with your former, more confident self? Or do you regret not setting boundaries earlier in your relationship? If so, you're probably Unhealthy Beta.

At times, you may feel more like a prisoner than a partner. You don't feel like you have a vote in life's major decisions, and you've learned it's easier to "go along and get along" than stand up for what you want or need. True connection, intimacy, and respect are replaced by eggshells, land mines, and self-doubt.

By identifying if you are Unhealthy Beta in any area of life, you gain an opportunity to reclaim your sense of self. As you come more fully back into your empowerment, you also increase the intimacy and connection in your relationship.

Unhealthy Beta is where "service" (sacrifice) begins to erode self-respect. Unhealthy Beta's are still working to earn or prove their worthiness, and will serve at the expense of themselves. As I mentioned above, this tends to be a slow fade. The qualities that were initially attractive to Alpha have been capitalized on, taken for granted, or pushed to the extreme (consumed). **This is not to blame**

Alpha. It's to empower you to know that regaining your sense of self is 100% your responsibility.

It's not uncommon for Unhealthy Betas to reflect back on their happier days when they were a stronger version of themselves. The chart below illustrates that fade.

In the beginning you were...	Now, you've become...
Supportive	Exhausted
Excited for Alpha's potential	Envious of Alpha's purpose
Optimistic for your future together	Left behind and feeling lost
Confident and Capable	Insecure and Uncertain

Some spouses of Unhealthy Betas feel like as a couple, they can no longer relate to one another. They may feel bored or uninterested in daily connection and conversation, heightening Unhealthy Beta's sense of feeling lost and uncertain. It's also not uncommon for spouses of Unhealthy Betas to *wish* their partner (Unhealthy Beta) would push back on them. They have grown tired of the ease at which their partner obliges. They're looking for a challenge and obligatory appeasing isn't cutting it.

There are two types of Beta on the Unhealthy side of the spectrum: Solo Beta and Shell Beta.

Solo Beta

Solo Betas betray *themselves* in order to support their partner. This can happen when they feel lost from who they are or what they need, so it's easier to focus on their partner or kids.

A Solo Beta will misplace blame on others for not prioritizing her in the same way she has prioritized them. She doesn't recognize that the sense of betrayal or neglect she feels stems from her own self-neglect.

This causes her to feel increasingly lonely and disconnected from others. She begins to withdraw from outside friends and family and stays in surface level conversations to avoid sharing the emptiness and disappointment she is experiencing at home.

Solo Betas are governed by loneliness as they keep pouring into others, hoping one more act of service may finally earn them love and respect. Solo Beta becomes overly concerned with keeping her partner happy while her own personal resentment continues to build. There are occasional but limited opportunities to pursue her own needs or desires. Even then, she may feel guilty for taking time for herself, or not know how to spend alone time in a way that excites her.

Shell Beta

The final stop on The Unhealthy Beta Spectrum is Shell Beta, named for the way it leaves a person feeling: like a shell of a human. Their body is there, but "they" are not. Their spirit is crushed and their core personality traits are a distant memory. They feel governed by fear, ensuring their choices do not upset their partner.

In the Shell Beta zone, there is little to no will left to communicate boundaries or desires. Shell Betas are laser focused on merely surviving. They likely experience exhaustion and brain fog as they navigate the day, using extreme mental gymnastics while working to avoid household upheaval.

Shell Betas are emotionally drained and physically exhausted in their relationship, but feel trapped. They work hard to manage their resentment because their partner keeps telling them, "You have an ideal life and have no reason to complain," but even managing that resentment feels exhausting now. Their inner voice is begging for freedom, but their logical mind cannot find a way.

> It is probable that there are other factors at play, such as low self-worth, depression, *anxiety, or a generalized experience of feeling like the "crazy one."*

ΩΩΩΩ

If you are a man in the Unhealthy Beta zone, your biggest priority is to work on your relationship with your own masculine energy. If your partner can't trust you to hold boundaries for yourself, she can't possibly trust you to protect her. Her rage with you is her sacred request to step into your masculine to powerfully and respectfully lead her.

UNHEALTHY BETA RECOVERY PLAN

If you've identified as Unhealthy Beta, you may be feeling a range of emotions from hopelessness to relief. But the emotion I find most common among Unhealthy Beta is resentment.

Resentment as an Invitation

You've bent over backwards accommodating everyone else, but no one has prioritized you and your needs and desires. You watch as your husband's life unfolds, seemingly miraculously, knowing it was your work behind the scenes that provided such a solid foundation. But now, you feel left behind, wondering what happened to your own life. Who wouldn't feel resentment after all that?

When Unhealthy Betas feel resentful, it can feel like your spouse should *stop* doing all of the activities that fill their cup to make you feel more at ease. This thinking suggests everyone reaching the lowest common denominator translates into increased happiness for all. From that perspective, you might recognize flawed thinking.

What if you considered your resentment as an invitation? What if everything you resented about your partner was actually an indicator of what you *wished* you had more of in your own life?

I suggest starting by taking inventory of all the resentments you harbor. Do you resent how much freedom your partner has? How many resources he has? The close relationships with friends and family? Their discipline in health and fitness? Consider these guideposts to reclaim your own sense of Self. Begin to carve out the time, energy, and commitment to restoring these factors in your own life.

The other hard truth about resentment is that often it can be misplaced on the spouse. Sometimes, the resentment you feel is not actually resentment toward your spouse but toward yourself. You're starting to recognize the ways you have betrayed yourself and your needs. By not prioritizing yourself, you've taught your partner that your needs aren't actually that important to you. Your spouse feels like the easy target, but claiming full responsibility for this empowers you to reclaim your choices so you can prioritize your own interests.

This will depend on another key strategy for Unhealthy Beta: Boundaries.

Boundaries are Beautiful

Boundaries are often difficult for Betas to establish because it can erroneously feel like you are restricting the relationship. In reality, you are expanding the relationship because you are creating space for you to rise more fully, while creating a more sustainable relationship with greater longevity.

My favorite example of this is the glass. Imagine if you were to hold a pitcher of water over the counter. Now, you tilt that pitcher over, allowing the water to pour all over the counter. That water now becomes completely useless and has caused a big mess. Now take that same pitcher and pour the water into a glass. That glass is the boundary. It has restricted the water, but in that restriction, it has made the water drinkable.

Boundaries give your relationship form and function. Without them, you have a mess of a relationship with no utility and no promising future.

This is why it's so critical for your counterpart to achieve Healthy Alpha, so your boundaries don't feel like limitations or control but a path to longevity and mutual fulfillment in the relationship. HOWEVER, don't wait for your partner to achieve Healthy Alpha.

Set and hold your boundaries now before your resentment grows further.

Worthiness

At the root of overserving, overgiving, and overpleasing, is a lack of self-worth and self-love.

Where Unhealthy Alpha tries to protect the hole in his heart with walls and addictions, Unhealthy Beta tries to fill the hole in her heart with love from others. You can see how this creates a lose-lose romance for both, as neither person is feeling seen or honored for what they need.

You may have been conditioned by your parents to earn love and attention with good behavior. Or maybe you found the best way to fit in at school was to help others. Regardless of the reason, when we know better, we do better. Becoming your own best lover and serving your Self as fiercely as you serve others will begin to fill the hole in your heart. From that place, you naturally lose the need to sacrifice your Self for others. Setting boundaries becomes an act of love for your Self instead of an act of aggression against your partner.

The Titanium Rule

The Golden Rule says to treat others the way you want to be treated.

The Platinum Rule says to treat others the way they want to be treated.

The Titanium Rule says to treat yourself the way you want others to treat you.

This means taking full ownership that <u>how you treat yourself teaches others how to treat you</u>. **Going forward, you live by The Titanium Rule: treat yourself the way you wish your partner would treat you.** This is going to remind both of you of that confident woman you remember from your earlier days together.

As that remembrance of your true Self starts to come back on line, lean into her. Welcome her back and make room for her. Honor her. Delight her. Laugh, dance, and cry with her.

An entirely filled up, lit up You is the new goal. While that version of You becomes the magnet that draws your partner in and creates a space of attraction, desire, respect, and commitment—that's NOT why you're doing it. You're doing it for your Self—with yourself and by yourself. The upleveled relationship is simply a by-product.

This may come from recognizing that your fitness routine is the catalyst to your confidence. It may come from the sense of pride you feel when you host others in your home with such a great knack for entertaining. It may come from your expertise on all things child-rearing (legacy creation). It may be returning to a hobby you once loved, but abandoned as responsibilities grew.

Ultimately, it's the place where you set all the dials of life to "Favorite." It's creating your life so joyfully that you intentionally fill your time with all of the things that bring you joy.

This means you might give yourself an extra ten minutes each morning for great hair and makeup; or finding a quiet spot in your house to curl up with your favorite blanket and mug and read or journal or draw. It might be starting your day with your favorite playlist or podcast. It might be a dance party in the kitchen. Maybe it's lighting all your favorite candles just because; or wearing your favorite perfume, even if you're not leaving the house.

My late friend Sean Stevenson called this exercise the "When Life Works List." It's also referred to as a 10x10 (Ten by Ten). The 10x10 is 10 things you do every day by 10 a.m. They don't have to be big things. They have to be your favorite things. This is how you start to carve the path back to your most lit up Self.

What's possible for that woman? How does she respond to mistreatment or disrespect? How does she unapologetically prioritize herself?

Join me for a moment in envisioning what her relationship might look like—a relationship where Healthy Alpha and Healthy Beta are both so personally fulfilled that their connection to each other becomes the magnet that draws all of life's blessings to them. Their intimacy becomes the portal to continued expansion. Their interdependence explodes all of life's possibilities to such a huge extent that NOT standing for one another's independence becomes nonnegotiable.

Imagine bridging the gap between where you are now as individuals, and where you could be as a happy, thriving couple.

Our next chapter, Understanding Omega, will provide that roadmap.

I'm so excited to share this concept with you because it has been such a game changer for me. I was so befuddled in my relationships having crashed and burned with two polar opposite men, I knew there was something in me that needed a new approach. I needed to "become the one" that could attract and maintain a healthy relationship.

For me, the work on "becoming the one" was *not* about dialing in my habits, leveling up my persona, or making massive changes to attract The One.

For me, the work was forgiving my ego for leading me on a massive wild goose-chase for my ambitious "power couple" partner.

The bigger work was surrendering my ego to the heart and letting my heart call the shots.

Where the ego said, "powerful," the heart said, "present."

Where the ego said, "provider," the heart said, "protector."

Where the ego said, "strong jawline," the heart said, "something in his eyes that took a thousand years to get here."

Where the ego said, "respected by many," the heart said, "respects himself."

Where the ego said, "changed thousands of lives," the heart said, "changed his own life."

Ego said, "someone you can build an empire with." Heart said, "someone you can build a life with."

Where the ego said, "adventurous, chivalrous, and generous," the heart said, "damn straight!"

I have found this in my current partner, but more importantly, I have found the balance in myself to cast vision and hold boundaries. I've learned the delicate and necessary balance of my Alpha and Beta energy.

The Omega Framework will show you how to create this in your relationship.

Please click the QR code below to find The Alpha-Beta Domain sheet for total clarity on how this works in your relationship.

Chapter 3

INTRODUCING OMEGA

Omega is like a Healthy Beta, but with a juicy, spicy kick. It's also like Healthy Alpha, but with a softer, easier presence.

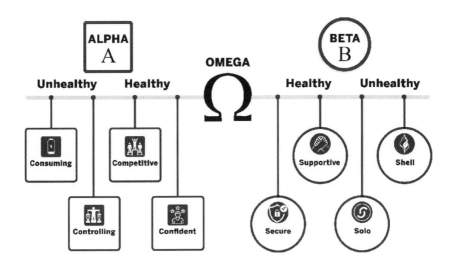

Omega is a perfect balance of Healthy Alpha and Healthy Beta. Omega can lead unapologetically and yield humbly. Omega has sharpened her intuition with a knowingness of when it's time to offer advice, hold boundaries, or be a raving fan.

Omega has a confidence or je ne sais quoi of her own that comes with not only supporting her partner, but also pursuing her own goals and dreams.

Omega is an invitation for women who are on The Beta Spectrum *and* women who are on The Alpha Spectrum.

For women on The Beta Spectrum, it offers a path to pursue her own goals without feeling like she needs to be hypermasculine and launch a huge business. She's satisfied with a pursuit that matches her desire, regardless of size or impact.

For women on The Alpha Spectrum, it offers relief from the exhaustion of always "being the man" in their relationships. Embracing Omega allows you to keep all of your power and all of your fire, but provides a respite from the constant grind of producing and initiating. It allows you to sink into your feminine for just long enough that you experience your man's leadership and the unfair advantage your feminine energy offers.

Oh sister, I want this for you. I want you to experience the next level of sorcery available to you when you access your feminine. I want the surrender of trusted relaxation and pleasure to consume you and have its way with you. And when you emerge from that euphoric stupor, I want you to be so damn impressed with how easy and delicious life has become. Friend, this is about more than wearing dresses and softer makeup. This is an inside job that yields ease, beauty, fun, pleasure, and trust.

For me personally, I found life as an Alpha female to be dry, brittle, and lonely. I found life as a Beta female to be unsteady, exhausting, and lonely. But striking that balance and learning how to harness my masculine energy and develop my feminine energy has changed the game for me in business and love.

For Beta women, this might mean harnessing your feminine and developing some masculine energy.

Omega is not an either/or game. It's an and/both. It's the place where two opposite things can be true at the same time. You're strong and soft. You're supportive and productive. You're silly and serious. You're in allowance and creation. You're giving and receiving. But most of all, it's magic and might.

I chose the name Omega for two reasons. First, Omega is the last letter of the Greek alphabet, allowing the most s p a c e from Alpha (the first letter of the Greek alphabet). When Beta gets sucked into the gravitational pull of Alpha, Beta loses her identity. Therefore, space (or an "unmeshing") is necessary to restore her identity.

Second, Omega broken down is O+Mega. Mega means great, mighty, important. To become Omega requires reclaiming a sense of self-importance, reprioritizing self-care, and honoring personal goals. This reclamation of self no longer depends on anyone else for a sense of self-importance. Omega stands on her own, yet can still love recklessly.

Alpha-Omega Integration Plan

While Alpha is still regarded as the leader, or the initiator and decider, it is actually Omega who stewards the possibilities. This dynamic creates a beautiful transfer of power between the two that establishes trust, intimacy, and mutual respect. The process works like this:

1) Alpha provides <u>options</u> for any given project or opportunity.

2) Omega identifies the <u>boundaries</u>, trusting that Alpha will honor those boundaries.

3) Alpha chooses the <u>highest possibility</u> based on those boundaries, trusting that Omega will yield and lean into Alpha's leadership.

In this exchange, partners will experience less resistance and more harmony. It starts to feel like a dance.

One way to understand this better is to take a page from the BDSM world. There was a valuable lesson in the *Fifty Shades of Grey* mania. It taught us that this kinky sexual practice forced **supreme**

communication. In the BDSM world, there is a dominant (dom) and a submissive (sub).

One would think that the dominant has all the power and the submissive has to oblige. Nothing could be further from the truth. The dom is the one that initiates or suggests the initial engagement, but it is actually the sub that has final say over what is and is not permissible, in reality giving the sub the most power with the final word.

All of this is communicated and agreed upon in advance, keeping expectations in check and allowing for a more present and engaging experience together.

Taking this back to The Alpha-Omega Framework, because Alpha is the initiator, Alpha will suggest a range of possibilities for any given domain. Omega will identify the boundaries, and Alpha will choose based on those boundaries—*without a passive-aggressive tone*—if the boundaries feel too restrictive.

This creates a synergy that allows Omega to exercise her voice and relax into the possibilities. Alpha maintains his sense of leadership and builds trust with his partner by honoring the boundaries.

Trust and respect are *feelings* that defy logical metrics. Establishing trust starts with immutable trustworthiness. This requires Alpha to be steadfast in honoring the boundaries. As Omega's trust and respect build, boundaries expand. As boundaries expand, possibilities grow. As possibilities grow, opportunities are captured. This is how true "power couples" create an amazing life together, while avoiding power struggles and deflated identities.

It takes deep, individual work for both parties to achieve this dynamic.

Alpha must take full ownership of staying on the healthy side of The Alpha Spectrum. This requires relinquishing control over his partner's day-to-day decisions, giving her the space to pursue her own identity. Alpha must honor this space, knowing that even if his partner's choices cause him anxiety and feeling lack of control, he trusts that her choices are cultivating a more fulfilled partner, and thereby a more dynamic relationship.

Beta must fully claim her rightful place as Omega by fully reclaiming her personal identity. She re-engages in her personal relationships with friends and family. She prioritizes time for her personal interests and hobbies. She develops her own goals and her own connection to purpose. She understands that purpose does not necessarily mean profession, and eases fully into the activities and callings that fill her proverbial cup. She identifies her boundaries, communicates them, and honors them in a consistent and respectful way.

Relationships with an Omega offer the entrepreneur growth in the business without the fear of growing apart. By stepping into Omega, partners of entrepreneurs enjoy a shared sense of growth and expansion alongside their entrepreneurial partner. The result is a relationship that enjoys the hallmarks of an Alpha-Omega relationship:

- safety & security

- freedom to be yourself

- relaxed & at ease

- shared vision of a bigger future

- spontaneous fun

- sense of humor

- trust & respect

- acceptance & allowance

- shared pace

- mutual growth

- self-sustaining chemistry

This is the relationship promised land I hear most of my couples describe. The Alpha-Omega Framework is the path to that shared connection. This is available to you. It's available to all of us with honest introspection and taking full ownership over how we're showing up as a spouse or partner.

It's about getting super present to all the ways your relationship supports you and constantly looking for more evidence that your relationship is a catalyst.

There are six key strategies necessary for growing The Alpha-Omega relationship. I call them The Presence Principles. Part II will outline these strategies.

Keep in mind that the strategies, without the bedrock of preserving The Alpha-Omega dynamic, will not yield the same result. They WILL make a positive impact, but ultimately, preserving the power dynamic just outlined is the most crucial part.

Also, please note that not every Beta will want to step into Omega. There will be some Betas that feel completely set free to simply maintain a Healthy Beta posture. That's acceptable as long as it's Beta's choice. Not everyone has the innate drive to kick it up a notch or become a producer. However, if rising to Omega isn't your jam, please hold the line at achieving and staying on the Healthy side of The Beta Spectrum.

PART II
THE PRESENCE PRINCIPLES

O nce you and your partner have committed to cultivating The Alpha-Omega dynamic, you'll need some strategies to support the upward trajectory.

Traditional relationship strategies, like better communication, date nights, and couples counseling are often not enough to get an entrepreneur or his spouse to the next level in their relationship. Entrepreneurs are their own unique breed, and their relationships require their own unique approach.

If you're an entrepreneur, you've probably had your spouse request more of your *presence*. For some, you get it. You spend most of your waking hours at work and even when you're home, you're thinking or talking about work. You can see her point about being more present, but you're not sure where to start.

For others, you can't figure out what the problem is. You're home most nights and weekends. You assess your work-life balance and can tally up plenty of hours when you're home and taking advantage of being your own boss. But your partner still feels like you aren't present.

What gives?

Here's where we've gone wrong: work-life balance reflects *time*—how many hours you spend at work versus how many hours you're home.

But as an entrepreneur, your work demands herculean amounts of *energy*. You've likely poured your best ideas, resources, talents, and capacity into the business. Your partner sees this output of energy has paid off with a thriving business, a team that respects you, and clients that love you.

Of course, it's only natural for her to want a fraction of that output put back into the relationship. She can probably see or feel an elevated version of your relationship with a portion of that energy being reinvested into her. After all, women are multipliers. If you give them a house, they make it a home. If you give them groceries, they make a meal. If you give them seed, they make a baby.

If all you're giving them is scraps of energy, the best they can offer back to you is a half-assed attempt at a partnership.

I know what you're thinking. "I'm already exhausted and now the only way to save my marriage is to double down on my output?"

No.

We're going to make your relationship your energy *generator*. You'll no longer have to be the one stoking all the flames to keep all the fires going. We're going to alchemize your personal life to be a multiplier, where the results can't help but spill over into your business.

Remember the Clydesdales and their 1+1=3 synergy?

What if we could do that for your marriage?

What if we could transform your love relationship to be so connected that it's as if you're seamlessly running life as a three-legged race? What if we could create so much synergy in your relationship that running the business becomes easier because it feels like the wind is always at your back.

All of this starts by recognizing that this synergy is one of the unfair advantages of a healthy love relationship that leads to greater success in business and in life. Sometimes this synergy happens instantly and automatically. Sometimes it develops over time. But rarely (or never) does it *sustain* itself over time. The strategies that follow will help you identify the six crucial areas entrepreneurs need to focus on in marriage to offset the demands of running a business.

Just like the dashboard of your car alerts you to the exact part of the vehicle that needs your attention; or how the EBITDA formula points to the exact areas of your business that increase it's valuation, these Presence Principles will help you focus on the areas of your marriage that will increase your intimacy and connection. Use these six strategies as checkpoints to see what's off and how you can fix it.

Some of these practices will be more relevant than others for you and your spouse.

Some of these practices will be more relevant to your spouse than they are to you.

Some of these practices will be more relevant to you than they are to your spouse.

A great relationship starts with being willing to meet a need that isn't yours. Keep that in mind if your partner expresses a need that you don't understand.

ΩΩΩΩ

The Presence Principles *are* gender nuanced. The first three: play, praise, and purpose are generally more important for men to experience in their relationships. The second three: provision, protection, and pursuit are generally more important for women to experience in their relationship. I encourage both people to attune to all six presence principles, with priority given to the principles that resonate most with you and your spouse.

Chapter 4

PLAY

Break the cycle of:
* Boredom
* Ruts
* Nothing in common
* Business/kids get the best of them; I get the rest of them

There's big work ahead, and we need the lighthearted, easy energetics of play to soften the proverbial soil. Play offers an easy shake-up to release the reigns of control and welcome both parties equally into the relationship. If we're going to create the relationship of our dreams, we need the creative energy that play generates.

Play is the opposite of struggle, depression, and work and offers the opportunity to engage in pleasurable activities with your lover. Play is where we see our partner in their best light, easing into the joy of carefree timelessness. Carefree timelessness is where love grows because we're "free to be," as evidenced by your dating days.

Your dating days likely consisted solely of play, allowing walls to be down and hearts to be open. You had a space of total positive expectancy and giving one another the benefit of the doubt. When we add marriage, in-laws, homes, kids, work, pets, other responsibilities, and stacking disappointments, play gets squeezed out the window. The magic and ease of play are replaced by the monotony and grind of life. It's no wonder we disconnect and fall into relationship ruts.

However, there's a bigger reason that play is important in relationships— *especially* for entrepreneurs.

Flow

Flow, or flow state, is a euphoric mental state where you feel and perform at optimum levels. Often referred to as "being in the zone," this is where all five of the "feel good" neurochemicals cascade throughout the nervous system. When a person is working in the sweet spot of their business, they achieve this peak state and become so completely laser focused, everything else falls away. Creativity and results skyrocket with minimum effort or exertion.

Spouses of entrepreneurs have to contend with the euphoric state of flow that their partners achieve in business. Compare that to the grind at home and it's no wonder work becomes so appealing! This contrast leaves entrepreneurs gravitating toward work, leaving loved ones feeling like "work gets the best of you and I get the rest of you." Stack this dynamic against a spouse who's at home and/or struggling with a lack of purpose and joy in her own life, and this disconnect is enough to sink even the strongest couples.

We need to counterbalance the euphoria of flow at work with the joy of play at home. This is one example of why we need to think about work-life balance in a new way.

When we talk about work-life balance, it's mostly in the context of time. It points to the notion that we need to protect some of our *time* for our family. But what about our energy? We rarely talk about balancing joy and euphoria with our families like we do with work. This is the function of play.

Often, couples will insist that they have plenty of play, telling me that they have date night once a week at their favorite restaurant. That's a good start, but it's not actually play. When you're at that dinner, what are you talking about? Likely it's work, the house, the kids, the family. . . .These conversations offer a nice opportunity to connect, but they don't rekindle the sense of attraction and intimacy we're working toward.

When you think of play, think of being active together. You're either engaged in an activity *together*, like pickleball, or you're playing alongside one another, like a paint-n-sip.

The goal is activity, where bodies are moving and there's a sense of co-creation. It creates plenty of space for spontaneous laughter and the opportunity to see your partner at ease. Being unencumbered and free-to-be is what you're working toward. This is where that sense of attraction and intimacy starts to come back on line.

From a biological perspective, when you're at play, you actually get an even more heightened response than you do from flow. Check out the chart below to see just how similar these two mental states are:

Neurochemical	Flow	Play
Norepinephrine	☑	☑
Dopamine	☑	☑
Anandamide	☑	☑
Serotonin	☑	☑
Endorphins	☑	☑
Oxytocin		☑

As you can see, play releases the same neurochemicals that flow does, but it also kicks in the love hormone, oxytocin.

Oxytocin, serotonin, and endorphins are all social bonding chemicals, so anytime you experience play with another person, there is a biological connection that is formed. This might explain why you feel more connected to your friends than your spouse at times—because friendships are heavy on the play and light on the grind.

Take some time to identify how you and your partner play best together. You might think back to your dating days for inspiration. Or perhaps it's time to honor the new individuals you've both grown into and make some space for trying new hobbies.

Don't panic if it feels like you no longer share the same interests. This is actually a great opportunity to expand the territory you two can cover as a couple. If you can hold space for your differences as life-expanders instead of relationship-destroyers, you may find even more fulfillment in your relationship.

For instance, you may have a new affinity for kayaking. And your partner may have an interest in disc golf. Now you actually have two hobbies you can do together, instead of both of you having only one individual pursuit.

Take turns alternating between one another's hobbies. Keep in mind that the purpose of sharing one another's hobbies is to help rekindle the romantic bond you share and to inject your shared lives with more play than work.

Steven Kotler, one of the leading experts on flow, shares some triggers that help evoke that euphoric state of flow. Keep these in mind as you think about which activities you and your partner might explore together:

- outdoor, novel environments

- varying degrees of risk (you might alternate between high and low risk if you and your partner have different risk tolerance)

- clear goals

- intrinsic motivation (you do it for love, not money)

- equal participation

- deep embodiment (the doer and the doing become one)

- open communication

- clear, immediate feedback (allowing to course-correct if necessary)

Sex Lives Here

Clients often ask me which Presence Principal sex falls under. The answer is all of them, but primarily it lives in Play.

Many entrepreneurs are hypersexual. Most spouses of entrepreneurs feel like they can't keep up with their partner because his desire for sex is so intense. This disparity leaves the entrepreneur feeling rejected, and the spouse feeling like every conversation, every touch, every interaction is going to lead to sex. She tempers her interactions with him to keep a safe enough distance that won't give him the wrong idea that she's up for sex at that moment. This contributes to the disconnect between partners.

My favorite resource to help bridge this gap is The Erotic Blueprint™ by Miss Jaiya. Just like The Five Love Languages™ help us understand how both partners give and receive love, The Erotic Blueprint™ does that for sex. It identifies five different types of sexual superpowers. Understanding what works for you versus what works for your partner helps bridge the sexual gap between you. This helps increase the frequency of sex by ensuring your spouse enjoys the type of sex that's on offer.

You can learn your type by taking a quiz at missjaiya.com.

To that end, reintegrating nonsexual touch is an important step for both parties to begin healing from any physical//sexual droughts that may have crept in.

A Child's Testimony of Playful Parents

Too often, couples use their children as a reason they have let date nights become a relic of their dating days. I would like to share the value of couples who play, from the perspective of a child.

When I was a child, I had a babysitter <u>every</u> Saturday night, without fail. I remember going shopping with my mom at Contempo Casuals so she was always on trend for her dates with my dad. My dad always wore Old Spice, a collared shirt, and crisp slacks so he looked great for my mom.

As they got ready for their date, I would trounce around the house in my mom's white, iridescent high heels, pretending I was the one heading out on the town. They legit went out dancing together every weekend. When they got home in the wee hours of the morning, they always came in to check on me in my bed. As a child, I loved knowing they were back home. As an adult, I'm so glad they left in the first place.

And every year they took an incredible vacation without my brother and me.

They never put one another down in front of us.

They didn't get bogged down in silly details or drama.

They put their marriage above their kids.

I'm so glad they did.

There was an air of ease around our house. And possibility. And adventure. And love. I often say that I had a perfect childhood, and their commitment to each other is the reason.

For additional resources on Play, please click the QR code below for a free download to get even more clear about adding Play to your relationship.

Chapter 5

PRAISE

Break the cycle of:
* Not feeling appreciated
* Criticizing
* Unrealistic expectations
* Lack of intimacy

One of my favorite definitions of intimacy is Into-Me-You-See. This brings me to one of the highest leverage points for improving any relationship: The Compliment-to-Criticism Ratio.

When you look at your partner, are you seeing their magic? Their mundane? Or their mania?

As I've already stated, strengths and weaknesses are buy-one-get-one. And in romantic relationships, it's the traits that initially attracted us to our partner that fade into the qualities we end up disliking later on. Sometimes, a gentle reminder to shift your perspective can be enough to get back on track.

Other times, it takes deep reflection and self-awareness to turn this dynamic around. For this, you can examine your Marriage Scorecard. The Marriage Scorecard is the mental tally you keep in your head of all *your points*, but your *partner's penalties*.

Most often, by the time you reach for that mental scorecard, you've already passed the threshold of being more critical than complimentary and you're simply looking to build your case. We have the Reticular Activator System (RAS) to thank for this.

> The RAS (Reticular Activating System) is a complex network of neurons that acts like a filter in our brain. This helps us decide what is important to pay attention to. It gathers information from our environment and decides what we should focus on. For instance, if you sense that you are in danger, it helps you pay attention to survival. If you're shopping for a new car, it helps you assess the qualities of all the cars around you.

When the RAS activates in your marriage, it looks to build evidence to support the story you have about your partner. For example, if you start to mentally build the case that your partner is selfish, your brain will work to find evidence supporting that belief. Everything they do will be chalked up to being selfish. Until you choose a new, positive story about your spouse, your mind will keep working to build evidence supporting your partner's selfishness.

Pay Attention to The Compliment-to-Criticism Ratio

This concept is especially important for entrepreneurs because, just like they can achieve flow at work, they also likely get more praise, appreciation, and respect at work. This continues to stack the scales for the entrepreneur to gravitate toward work because he is revered there.

There, he's driven, creative, passionate, well-connected, smart, and a great delegator. But at home those same traits can show up as controlling, chaotic, emotional, distracted, aloof, and even lazy. This is the classic case of where entrepreneurial traits are celebrated at work, but they are challenging at home.

Occasionally this causes an entrepreneur's ego to overinflate. The spouse grows weary of all the adoration her "amazing" husband receives at work, knowing his bright light casts the largest shadow at home. She knows the last thing he needs is another "yes" person around, and works to keep him in check. She intentionally withholds her praise and resentment sets in for both of them. "Why can't she respect me as much as everyone else does?" he wonders.

One thing I wish every spouse of an entrepreneur knew is that he would gladly trade in all of the applause in the world for your appreciation, in a heartbeat. It'd be a no-brainer for him. Most entrepreneurs emphasize that earning their wife's affirmation is

> a primary driver for their success. They work tirelessly for an "atta boy" from her. When instead he's met with criticism, he starts to resent her.

Another reason a spouse withholds praise is she begins to recognize he is outgrowing her. Some spouses report intentionally withholding praise out of fear that if she compliments her husband, he'll recognize he has nothing to compliment her back on. This causes some degree of withdrawal, widening The Ambition Gap.

Conversely, if the spouse is in a more traditional employment role or doesn't work outside the home, she may be feeling perpetually unappreciated. If she's completely devoid of recognition outside the home, it's crucial for the entrepreneur to speak life into his partner. Hold space and positive expectancy for her to rise to meet you.

Remember, what we appreciate, appreciates. Keep speaking into the parts of her that you adore—her unique talents and gifts—and invite her into your growing world. Speaking into her contribution and uniqueness will build intimacy and shared growth.

There's no universally perfect ratio when it comes to compliments::criticism, so long as your relationship is more affirming than it is condemning. Your partner might need two compliments for every criticism. You might need ten compliments for every criticism. It's okay to share this number with your partner, and learn what they need in return.

Receiving Praise

One of the most common challenges couples report in this area is the rejection of praise when it's offered. One spouse will insist they work really hard to compliment their partner, only to be met with, "No I'm not." For example, "Honey, you're one of the smartest people I know!" is met with, "No I'm not. You're around smart people all day. You're just trying to be nice."

This deflection of praise is often well-intended, hoping to maintain humility, but it comes across as rejection.

Receiving your partner's praise is a crucial way of building intimacy. There are ways you can receive praise and still maintain humility. Next time you can try some responses like this:

- Thank you, honey. That means so much coming from you!

- Thank you for seeing the best in me.

- Thanks babe! I've been working really hard at that!

- Awe, you're making me blush.

Effective Feedback

When it comes to praise, it's equal parts how often we affirm our partner, and how we address bad behavior when we need to. Of course, there will be times when criticism or negative feedback is necessary to address a challenging behavior. How we *give and receive* that feedback is critical.

The best way to share negative feedback is to stay focused on your feelings when challenging behavior arises. Instead of saying, "You act like a total jerk every time you don't get your way," try, "When we're making big decisions together, I feel a little scared to disagree with you. Opinions that aren't yours seem to really frustrate you and I don't know how to handle your anger when that happens."

If your partner gives you feedback or requests a change of behavior, how do you respond? Are you open and curious, willing to meet a need that isn't yours? Or do you unleash the wrecking ball, leveling your partner and the relationship each time your imperfections are called out?

Receiving negative feedback is just as important as receiving praise. It helps establish necessary boundaries to perpetuate a healthy relationship. Offering a punishment that doesn't fit the crime is going to keep your partner on eggshells, perpetuating the Unhealthy Alpha-Unhealthy Beta dynamic.

As humans, we can either create or defend. If you're busy defending yourself or your position, you lose the ability to create a solution. Staying open, curious, and compassionate will help you both reach a solution-based state instead of the downward spiral of defensiveness.

Embracing Your Differences

As I stated earlier, the traits that initially attracted us to our partner can often turn into our biggest grievances later in the relationship. Initially, we recognize these differences as a perfect complement to our lives. As life progresses, we start to feel like those differences hold us back. We may even go as far as believing that our partner would be so much better if only they were more like us.

If you can remember to appreciate your differences as providing balance instead of proving incompatibility, it will be exponentially easier to maintain The Compliment-to-Criticism Ratio.

Instead of measuring your differences as liabilities, count them as expanders. Pairing your skillset *next* to (instead of versus) your partner's, you'll likely slip from frustration straight into gratitude for how much your differences expand the territory you can cover as a couple.

Avoid Past-casting

We often evolve faster than our partner's perception of us. The same is true for your partner. This means that your partner may be evolving out of old habits, but you're holding him hostage to mistakes of his past. It may have been months or even years since he made a poor decision, but you still hold him to the standard of who he was before, discrediting his growth.

Releasing one another from mistakes of the past will help to rebalance the scales of The Compliment-to-Criticism Ratio.

Potent Praise & Devastating Criticism

There are a few areas of "personhood" that pack more punch when it comes to recognition. Consider all the aspects of your spouse that are "factory installed":

- their health, wellness, and physical attributes

- their intelligence and personal interests

- their emotional set point

- their spirituality

- their character or personality

- their sexuality

These areas offer deeper intimacy when appreciated and respected. But they can destroy intimacy when criticized.

Essentially, these areas comprise *who* your partner is. Criticism in these areas likely validates your partner's deepest insecurities, while appreciation of these qualities helps them feel seen at the deepest levels.

For some partners, this level of recognition right out of the gate may be too intimate. Working together to find the right level of recognition will require your open hearts and communication to find the right level.

A great question to facilitate this is knowing what compliment means the most to you and your spouse. What's the one thing that he or she could say to you that would melt your heart and make you weak in the knees, feeling truly seen at a core level?

Sharing that insight with one another allows both of you to have a lens for getting straight to the heart of the matter. It also clues you into the times your partner is in that space, and knowing that recognition is important in those times.

In other words, if your spouse tells you the best compliment you can give her is how devoted she is to her spiritual growth, you now know that when she's in her devotion, an extra nod after she's been in practice goes a long way.

For additional resources on Praise, please click the QR code below for a free download to get even more clear about adding Praise to your relationship.

Chapter 6

PURPOSE

> Break the cycle of:
> * The Ambition Gap
> * No shared goals
> * No shared vision of a bigger future
> * Loneliness in marriage

This one's a biggie, and one of the foundational areas entrepreneurial couples need to get clear on as individuals before they have a common purpose as a couple.

Some spouses of entrepreneurs report feeling a sense of "purpose envy." They watch their partner head to work with an invigorating sense of purpose, questioning if they'll ever feel so passionate about anything.

Purpose is deeply personal, and it's important to allow space for each person to identify and pursue their own purpose. Most spouses of entrepreneurs express a desire to pursue a greater purpose in life, but feel stuck at where to begin. They share frustrations like these:

- Our flexibility is really important to us; it would be hard to get a job with how often we travel.

- We committed to raising our kids ourselves; I have to wait until my kids are grown to pursue my own passion.

- My husband is so committed to his work; where is more passion and purpose going to fit?

Remember, purpose is deeply personal and sometimes, it's seasonal. Purpose doesn't have to be a profession. You may be in a season of life where your purpose is pouring into your family's legacy via your children or aging parents. As long as you're doing it with intention and fulfillment, that counts as purpose. If it lights you up and puts a pep in your step, it counts as purpose. If it puts a lump in your throat and a tear in your eye? That's purpose.

If you're in a season of feeling like you're ready to expand and searching for more purpose, I have two key points for you:

1) If you're feeling the pull to something bigger, rest assured that "something" is also seeking you. Not everyone is purpose-driven or purpose-seeking. If you have that stir for more, trust it as a calling or an invitation. Pursuing that purpose probably won't be a clear line. It will likely lead you to unexpected places, but isn't that the point? To find *yourself* after feeling lost?

2) Full disclosure: this one may frustrate a driven entrepreneur. But purpose is personal and this advice isn't for an already purpose-driven person; it's for the seeker. That advice is to dabble. Start pushing on doors and see if any of them swing open. This is one area where it's okay not to finish what you start. If you think you may be into volunteering at an animal shelter, then you get there and don't feel that spark, don't waste more time there trying to make it work. Move on to the next pursuit until you find "it."

One of my favorite stories of this is my client Robyn. She and her husband own an equestrian training business. Her husband is the "face" of the company and she works behind the scenes making all the magic happen. When she reached out to me, there was one request: "I want to find something that's my own. Our company is great, but I want something that's mine and fills my proverbial buckets."

I began with the dabbling advice and, together, we identified a few preliminary activities that were in the general arena of pursuits that interested her. We started with some breathwork training that she could offer the women in her community. She got to work writing the training, offering, and executing. She liked it, but it wasn't "it." Next we moved on to the Brené Brown certification she had attained earlier. "Maybe I could do something like that?" She started putting the program together, but wasn't feeling the pull. Soon, working on it felt more like a chore than a charge, so we scrapped it. The goal wasn't to launch a successful program. The goal was to find her purpose, so she felt complete permission to pivot when she sensed she was on the wrong path.

Finally, almost by accident, she got introduced to ice baths and felt the immediate pulse of purpose! This was nowhere on her radar when we started working together. But by knowing what purpose *didn't* feel like it, she knew it when she did find it.

Purpose is landing square in the center of your heart. It's when you reach resonant frequency and have a knowingness you're in the right place.

Resonant frequency is a term in physics used to describe when an object vibrates with maximum amplitude. Without getting too technical, I explain it in the context of a sports car. Let's take the Bugatti for example. The Bugatti is designed to reach speeds in excess of 120mph. At that speed, the vehicle is practically silent and steers effortlessly. Car and driver become one because the vehicle is doing what it was designed to do. That's resonant frequency. However, take that same car down Main Street at 35mph, and it's loud and clunky, every bump disrupts the entire cabin, and steering is hard and awkward. That car is no longer doing the thing it was designed to do and has fallen out of resonant frequency, making it an unpleasant experience for car, driver, and all those within earshot.

As an added bonus, Robyn finding her own purpose and reaching resonant frequency ended up helping their primary business. She posted a video of her ice bath, and it went viral! That video brought more leads to their business AND created a value-add to their existing client base. Sharing her passion with their clients helped them uplevel their own lives with this game-changing practice.

> If you haven't explored the benefits of ice baths or cold plunges yet, let this be your que! This cold water immersion offers tons of benefits to mind, body, and soul. It increases dopamine production by 250%, reduces inflammation in the body, and offers a psychological boost by overcoming hard challenges.

Step Away from the Whiteboard

When a spouse is purpose-seeking and starts to express a desire for deeper personal fulfillment, it's very common for the entrepreneur to rush to the nearest whiteboard and start mind-mapping a new business possibility. It typically goes something like this:

Spouse: "I need something that's just for me. I think I'd like to try the new yoga studio in town."

Entrepreneur: "OMG! That'd be so great! Maybe you could get your instructor certification! And we could open your own studio! I bet you could have three locations in the next three years. . . ."

The spouse feels deflated and decides she should have kept her idea to herself. She doesn't want to run a full blown business; she just wants more significance in her life. The entrepreneur feels rejected because he just wants her to trust his vision. He sees so much potential in her and wishes she saw the same for herself.

The best advice I can offer here is to embrace the dabble. It may drive you nuts that she starts so many hobbies but none of them stick. That's okay. It's part of the discovery process. Release attachment to what you think her purpose is, and allow it to unfold with her, for her, and by her.

Also, remember not everyone wants to have their own business. That doesn't make them unmotivated. That makes them clear. And let's face it—it makes them sane.

Shared Purpose

As each person gets clearer on their own individual purpose, it will be important for the couple to define a shared purpose together. Pick a point out on the time horizon. It could be two, ten, twenty, or even fifty years from now. What's true when you see yourselves out there together?

Have you established a foundation together? Have you stepped foot on each continent together? Have you held each other accountable to your becoming your best selves through all seasons of life? Have you become bold and courageous in your communication?

Dig deep on what you believe the purpose of your relationship is. That purpose will fuel you as you encounter setbacks in your relationship and life. As disappointments in the relationship mount, it will be important to get back to your purpose.

Every relationship goes through cycles. Most couples are constantly up against the same problem in their relationship. This is where having a solid purpose will help pull you through. When you get into the weeds of your relationship, and you measure that problem against your vision, does it still feel like a problem? For example, if you and your spouse keep finding yourselves arguing about how much time to spend with in-laws, but your purpose is to learn the depths of love with one another, does fighting about in-laws still feel relevant?

Re-anchoring to your purpose during the down-swings of your relationship cycles will help keep perspective on what you're fighting for.

Balancing the Scales

It's okay if you don't have a big, huge, world-changing purpose together. Some couples identify the purpose of their relationship is simply to balance one another out.

Use the circles below to help you identify the ideal balance between you and your spouse.

Together, you and your spouse can decide how much overlap you have in one another's lives. There is no right or wrong, but I tend to advise against the extremes.

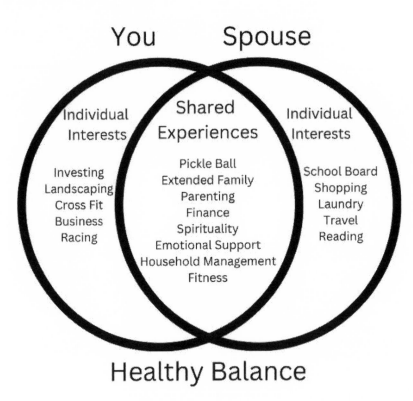

Some couples like very little overlap, simply sharing parenting and financial responsibilities while enjoying strong individual autonomy. This is called a parenting marriage and some couples choose this as a financial-lifestyle solution. However, this arrangement will not yield any results on the intimacy scale.

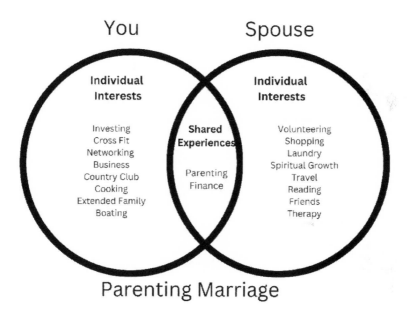

Other couples like an extreme amount of overlap, leaving minimal pursuits to each individual. This gets into co-dependent territory and some couples choose this route instead of working to heal individual wounds. This arrangement offers extreme intimacy, but often stifles individual expansion necessary in sustaining a healthy relationship.

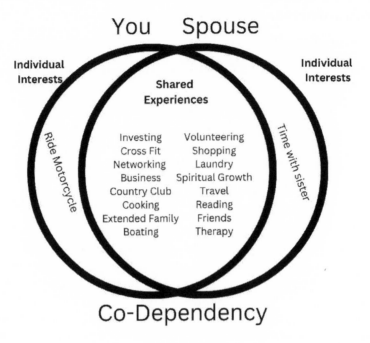

You   Spouse

Individual Interests

Shared Experiences

Individual Interests

Ride Motorcycle

Time with sister

Investing   Volunteering
Cross Fit   Shopping
Networking   Laundry
Business   Spiritual Growth
Country Club   Travel
Cooking   Reading
Extended Family   Friends
Boating   Therapy

Co-Dependency

Click the QR code below for an exercise to help get extra clear about balancing the scales and which activities you prefer to share, and which you prefer to keep as individuals as you add more Purpose to your relationship.

Coach's Notes from the Trenches

Because entrepreneurs tend to be more purpose-driven, they can fall into the trap of believing they would have a more fulfilling marriage with someone who was equally ambitious. This is The Ambition Gap I referred to in the Introduction that has swallowed countless entrepreneurial couples.

Couples who are equally purpose-driven often experience greater challenges in romantic relationships long-term. Both are so committed to their individual purposes that neither person is overly excited about compromising on that purpose to accommodate a relationship. If one partner does end up yielding to support the relationship, resentment can take hold.

Of course, that doesn't mean that two ambitious people can't have a healthy relationship. They can. But if you're feeling underwhelmed in your current relationship and considering leaving for a more driven person, beware. The initial explosion of chemistry can end up being the same flame that burns the house down. Often, you end up trading one set of problems in for another.

Chapter 7

PROVISION

Break the cycle of:
* I'm your spouse, not your employee
* Lack of security
* Thinking you'd be better off alone

As an entrepreneur, if your sense of provision starts and stops with *financial* provision, it has probably left your spouse feeling more like an employee than a partner.

Remember, romantic partnerships are about doing life together. That requires varying degrees of emotional support, intellectual stimulation, spiritual leadership, social integration, parenting collaboration, and household management.

When entrepreneurs feel out of their element in any area, they divert to the tried-and-true practice of delegation. "This isn't my sweet spot. Can we find someone else to do this?"

For some things like landscaping or household cleaning, that's an entirely appropriate response that relieves both people. But when you self-select out of all areas of doing life together, you clip all the ties that weave the intimacy you're craving.

These areas of life are your opportunities to show up for your partner the same way you show up for your business. When you show up and are present in these areas, you communicate to your spouse that she gets the same priority as your business.

These dynamics are best understood through the story of Kevin and Jess. Kevin owns a successful wealth management practice and Jess is the Chief Happiness Officer at home with him and their three young kids.

Jess is a parenting ninja and runs the household like a finely tuned watch. She immerses herself fully into her kids each day, eager for Kevin to get home at night and offer support and adult companionship.

Except, every night when Kevin gets home, he's exhausted. His fuse is short and he snaps at her and the kids often. Jess stops expecting support from him and slowly edges him out of the parenting role, careful to protect herself and the kids from his outbursts and shutdowns. Eventually, she feels like a single mom with a stranger in her bed.

She resents Kevin. Being with the kids all day is lonely and exhausting, and by now Kevin is completely out of touch with their developing lives. Jess tells him how overwhelmed she feels with shouldering the entire household and parenting responsibilities on her own.

Kevin's response is always the same: "Why don't we just hire someone to help you?" So far, they've added an au pair, a housekeeper, and a personal assistant to help lighten Jess's load. But Jess's loneliness and discontent grows.

One day, Kevin confided in me, "Honestly, I think she's acting spoiled and entitled. We live a life that's bigger than we ever could have dreamed of. She's got more assistants than I do in my company. We take great vacations; we live in a great neighborhood; our kids are in private school; I've given her everything she's ever asked for and I just don't even feel like trying anymore because I think she's just incapable of being happy."

After a healthy pause, I asked him, "Kevin, what was the income level you hit that you out-earned all your problems?"

"What do you mean?" he responded.

"In your business," I continued, "what was the annual revenue you hit where all your problems went away? Was it your first six-figures? Your first million? Your first ten million . . ."

He chuckled. "No! Of course not. I still haven't hit it. I'm not following where you are going though."

"You can't out-earn her problems any more than you can out-earn your own problems. Because if money can fix it, it *isn't* a problem. You've been throwing money at this all these years, but she's not asking for more money. She's asking for YOU. She wants your presence, your interest, your engagement."

And this, my love, is where so many of my entrepreneur clients go wrong. They believe their role in the family starts and stops with financial provision.

As an entrepreneur, financial income is a key indicator of success, so of course you have full attention on it. But remember, your spouse likely has a story that the business gets the best of you and she gets the rest of you. When you presume your sole contribution is financial provision, it underscores that belief. Your spouse is counting on you to help build a life. She's counting on you to help with household management, parenting, extended family involvement, social engagements, and of course, her own emotional connection.

When you rely on your financial contribution as being your sole source of provision, she feels let down in many other areas. This, of course, can leave you feeling defeated. You work so hard to provide a life that most could only dream of—you can't help but feel unappreciated.

Your prime function in business may very well be revenue capture. However, as part of a family unit, your provision extends beyond the financial component. Your provision here requires provision of self.

I know you're exhausted. I know you shoulder an incredible burden at work. I know when you look at other husbands, you may see more typical 9–5 guys and think, "They get to be more involved at home because they don't have near the amount of stress and demands that I do." But I can promise you, if you can get present to your wife and her needs, you activate your most unfair advantage in business and life: a lit up woman who adores you and fuels your business growth.

When your partner feels your emotional provision, you activate her in a different way. You allow her to relax into her pleasure center. This allows you to come home to a woman who's at ease and joyful. In turn, you find yourself with a partner who truly respects and appreciates you.

And if there's one thing I know for sure, it's that the most confident, productive, and fulfilled entrepreneurs on the planet are the ones with a healthy, balanced, thriving love relationship that is locked and loaded and firing on all cylinders. This can't happen when your only contribution is financial.

How Spouses Contribute

Some spouses contribute with an income and benefits of their own from more traditional employment. For whatever it's worth, I've found this pairing to be one of the healthier models from a romantic perspective. What this couple gains in romantic compatibility is often traded for time-freedom and/or influence on the family. I offer this as a perspective to help weigh your options.

Other spouses contribute in the form of sweat equity. They're keeping life on the rails at home to sustain other key areas of life. This provides a strong home base and peace of mind to the entrepreneur—an invaluable contribution when preserving mental bandwidth is top priority.

This may seem like an archaic perspective, reminiscent of a 1950s *Good Housekeeping* article, but when a spouse's contribution is sweat equity, there are some things to keep in mind:

1) The danger of this dynamic is that the spouse may lose parts of her identity. Not every woman is built to be a domestic

goddess, and yet some will still choose to stay home to maximize time-freedom and pour into the family.

In this case, it's important for the spouse to be working on expanding her own capabilities—for her own personal fulfillment *and* to contribute to the couple's synergy. The goal here is for both people to experience the benefits and expansion their partnership offers.

2) This role is often dramatically undervalued.

Every calculation I've seen on the financial value of a stay-at-home spouse accounts for the various roles she plays (cook, nurse, chauffeur, teacher, spiritual leader, personal shopper, etc.). What doesn't get taken into account is the impact she has on her partner's confidence.

So, if you're the entrepreneur evaluating the ROI for being the sole financial provider, consider this domino effect: Your spouse is lit up, confident, and in her Omega energy on most days. This elevates the synergy in your partnership, causing you to feel more appreciated and confident. When you get to work, with all that confidence, what are you capable of in business? Could you double your results? Triple them? Ten-times them?

Often, there's a resounding "YES!" when I ask that question. That differential should be accounted for when trying to place a financial value on a stay-at-home partner.

3) This brings us back to point 1: ensuring the spouse stays true to herself and her own growth.

This may come in the form of increasing efficiency for running the house—*if* (and only if) she's lit up by being a domestic goddess. Or, it may mean that she's developing other talents that contribute to the couple or the household.

For example, maybe she's a social butterfly and getting more involved in women's groups helps expand the couples' social circle. Or maybe she's a craft maven and her contributions help bring the home environment to a new level. Or maybe she loves rabbit holes and her research has helped bring new resources to the family.

Regardless of the way she chooses to expand herself, the key is that it's *hers*. This is the way she's maintaining her identity and the pursuit that will keep her grounded in her Omega (or Healthy Beta) energy.

Outsourced Contribution

This doesn't mean that everything at home becomes the spouse's responsibility. As I've stated, there are certain areas that will require shared contribution from both the spouse and the business owner. There are also some activities that can be outsourced altogether.

If certain responsibilities—like house cleaning, grocery shopping, mundane errands, or laundry—cause the spouse considerable stress or disdain, I take a page from the entrepreneur's book and "delegate to elevate." The key here is to elevate.

If you're going to make the financial investment to outsource at home, there needs to be an ROI in the happiness and expansion of the spouse. In other words, if the spouse is alleviated from the housekeeping, say that clears up ten–twelve hours a week for her. How will those hours be spent to provide a sense of fulfillment that equates to a lit up spouse?

Taking that even further, how does having a fulfilled, lit up spouse translate to increased ROI for the business owner? If he's coming home most days to a spouse who's happy, energized, and present, *and* the house is clean, what does that do to his confidence?

This is the exact path to The Alpha-Omega relationship I outlined in Part I. It may cost a couple hundred dollars a month (or even a week) to create the space for the spouse to elevate. But my experience has shown that the ROI on a happier spouse increases exponentially in the entrepreneur's ability to grow the relationship and the business.

On the Financial Note

Money can be a sticky subject for entrepreneurial couples. Some spouses feel guilty for spending money if they don't work outside the house. Some spouses feel disempowered when they need to ask for permission to spend. For these reasons, I like the "yours, mine, and ours" accounts.

"Yours, mine, and ours" accounts allow both people to have access to their own money for guilt-free spending and some degree of privacy. To make this work, the lion's share of income goes into the "ours" account to pay all household, lifestyle, and shared expenses. But both people also have their own individual accounts to spend at-will. This way, if either person wants to take a weekend getaway with friends, they can do so without it causing stress on the relationship. Or, if they want to spend money on a gift for one another, they can do so at their discretion. Obviously, this approach requires mutual trust and respect, which is what we're working toward.

I also like this approach because it keeps both parties in check to ensure money isn't being weaponized in the relationship—an important strategy to keep Alpha on the Healthy end of The Alpha Spectrum.

ΩΩΩΩ

We are in an era when, for the first time in modern history, many women earn more income than their husbands. While this is a win for women in the workforce, it presents challenges at home for many couples.

If this is true in your household, there are a couple of tips for both of you:

If your wife earns more than you—celebrate her! If she doesn't have an issue with it, don't make one. If it makes you uneasy, challenge your own insecurities around that, as it's not her responsibility to shield you from feeling triggered by her success. As long as you're showing up and providing in other ways, you're still preserving your masculine role and allowing her to ease into her feminine. Don't let her income define how powerfully you're willing to show up for her in other areas.

If you earn more than your husband—don't be a dick about it! Money is a tool that provides options, *not a measurement of personal superiority.* If you happen to be the one bringing more income into the family, don't make it a control mechanism that forces your man into submission. Allow him to lead you in other ways. When women create from their feminine, they are always more powerful.

For additional resources on Provision, please click the QR code below for a free download to get even more clear about how to increase Provision in your relationship.

Chapter 8

PROTECTION

Break the Cycle of:
* Business gets the best of you; I get the rest of you
* The only thing you care about is yourself
* Avoiding landmines and walking on eggshells

The entrepreneurial journey is riddled with risk. Entrepreneurs and their families are exposed to financial risks, social risks, and sometimes even risks to personal safety. All of this is directly opposed to the primary need of women in relationships: security.

Creating a sense of security in an entrepreneurial household is one of the surest ways to increase the harmony and intimacy in your relationship. At the end of the day, every woman wants to know she is worth fighting for and that her general well-being is paramount in your life.

The gestures of protection are small but mighty. Many of the spouses I work with swoon at some basic ideas like the following:

- making sure there is always gas in her car

- checking her tire pressure

- making sure the doors are locked each night

- surveying the environment for unforeseen threats

- walking on the sidewalk in between her and traffic

- having life insurance or investments in place to ensure her peace of mind in case of your unexpected passing

- keeping cash liquid to ensure the family is safe if the business has a setback

These are tiny gestures that convey a huge message—their safety and well-being are top of mind. Even the strongest, most independent women I know appreciate when their partner can keep pace with them and work to offer gestures of protection. It's not because they aren't capable of doing it themselves, but because they appreciate knowing they are valued, respected, and cherished by their partners.

Protection can also go beyond physical safety. Some partners are looking for emotional protection from intrusive in-laws or siblings. Some partners are looking for backup against unruly children. Others are seeking solace from social ill-will that may result from unpopular but necessary business decisions.

Learning what your partner is looking for by way of protecting them will give you clarity on this principle.

Protection vs. Control

As you consider ways to offer protection to your partner, your intentionality will be crucial. Remember, protection can also be a noble way of saying "control," so your intentions will be paramount. Here's the filter you can use to ensure you're staying on the healthy side of protection:

1) Did my partner request protection from this?

2) Is she actually in danger? Or do I just have fear that I'll lose control over something?

One of the most memorable stories of this comes from Ryan and Ashley. Ryan was an up-and-coming tech entrepreneur with two breakthrough products hitting the market. He had more and more investors coming on and his financial success had leveraged his wife, Ashley, to stay home with their four-year-old daughter.

Ashley had a great eye for fashion and expressed a desire to start her own personal shopping business. She went from quiet and subdued to passionate and confident every time she talked about how much she loved styling her friends. "It's so cool to see how changing just a few pieces completely transforms them into a stylish, confident woman! They've all told me how much better they feel, and I really feel like I could make a business out of this!"

As Ashley's posture opened up and her excitement grew, Ryan became agitated. I asked him how he felt about Ashley's aspirations and he said, "Yeah, she is great with fashion, but it's not a business. She doesn't understand how many other things she's going to have to do if she makes a business out of it, and I'm just trying to *protect* her from making a huge mistake."

From my work with them, I knew Ryan was Unhealthy Alpha and Ashley was Unhealthy Beta, and this scenario was just one example. Ryan was working to "protect" Ashley from making mistakes (this was one of many), and Ashley didn't trust herself enough to push back or stand up for herself.

The resolution with them was to get Ryan to recognize where this deep need for control was coming from (profound childhood trauma), and to help Ashley develop her self-worth so she respected herself enough to hold boundaries and trust her gut.

As Ryan loosened the grip on Ashley's decisions, Ashley emerged with more and more confidence. She did set up a hobby business as a personal shopper and grew a decent following. However, her real win was feeling like her full self. She was more confident in her own life. She no longer felt like she had nothing to offer aside from being "Ryan's wife". Now, instead of just feeling like Ryan's tagalong, she got to contribute with her own ideas and passion. She had an identity of her own and that was worth more than her business endeavor.

Protection from Your Anger

Perhaps the most important aspect of protection is your self-control over your own bad mood and temper. I can't tell you how many clients insist they have the area of protection on lockdown. "We're armed, we live in a gated community, we have dogs and state-of-the-art security systems."

But what they have failed to recognize is that the biggest threat in their spouse's life is their unchecked anger or untreated mental health challenges. The exterior of the home is, in fact, rock solid. It's the outbursts, stonewalling, and gaslighting that's happening inside the home that causes the most harm.

In short, Unhealthy Alphas believe their role is to protect themselves from outside threats. Rarely do they recognize that the biggest threat to themselves and their family is their own unchecked ego and unaddressed trauma, which can wreak havoc on the family from inside the home. This is where the work to maintain a Healthy Alpha posture can change everything.

How the Spouse Offers Protection

One of the ways spouses offer protection is helping to protect the entrepreneur's confidence. As Dan Sullivan says, "Confidence is the electricity of life, and the most important job of the entrepreneur is to always protect their confidence."

As the most important person in your partner's life, you have a tremendous impact on their confidence. This goes back to how important praise and affirmation is in your relationship.

Of course, all of this is presuming your partner is in Healthy Alpha. When your partner is Healthy Alpha, offering this protection of confidence will be easy and authentic. If your partner is Unhealthy Alpha, it is not your responsibility to continue enabling his fragile ego. It is his responsibility to do the healing work toward becoming Healthy Alpha.

For additional resources on Protection, please click the QR code below for a free download to get even more clear about how to increase Protection in your relationship.

Chapter 9

PURSUIT

Break the cycle of:
* Boredom in marriage
* Curiosity about what else is out there
* Taking one another for granted
* Loneliness in marriage

To love someone long-term is to attend a thousand funerals of the people they used to be.

The people they're too exhausted to be any longer.

The people they don't recognize inside themselves anymore.

The people they grew out of, the people they never ended up growing into.

We so badly want the people we love to get their spark back when it burns out; to become speedily found when they are lost.

But it is not our job to hold anyone accountable to the people they used to be.

It is our job to travel with them between each version and to honor what emerges along the way.

Sometimes it will be an even more luminescent flame.

Sometimes it will be a flicker that disappears and temporarily floods the room with a perfect and necessary darkness.

—*Attributed to Heidi Priebe*

This is the essence of pursuit: to travel with one another through all the versions of Self that emerge along the way. It's to continually hunt down the best version of yourself while holding space for your partner to do the same.

Pursuit means you're perpetually showing desire for your spouse and desire to continually do life together. It's always casting the vision of what the next chapter of your lives will look like together. It's prioritizing one another and initiating bids of connection.

Sometimes this means you're running life together in that three-legged race—perfectly in sync, leaning fully into one another and running in the same direction.

Other times it feels like a game of leap-frog, alternating between growth and lag states, but always bouncing off of one another and propelling one another forward.

Sometimes it will feel like a wheelbarrow race—like you're the one carrying all the weight, steering the course, and asking the bare minimum of your partner bearing his or her own weight.

And still other times it will feel like Marco Polo. You can't see your partner, but you know they're there. It feels like every few months you lose track of one another and fall out of sync. You may even question if you two belong together. You call out their name, uncertain if you want them to respond. After a few seconds they meagerly eek out their name and you have hope that there's still a shot in the dark. You start to reconnect and end up coming out stronger on the other side.

This is pursuit: to keep initiating desire for your partner, regardless of where you are in the relationship cycle.

One age-old question with pursuit is how to maintain the thrill of the hunt in a long-term relationship. Really, it's as simple as the ABCs: Always Be Chasin'!

Another word for pursuit is initiation.

Pay attention to where you've become accustomed to your partner initiating and switch things up by initiating in that area for a change. So if your partner is always the one that makes advances for sex, you offer pursuit by making the first move for a change. Or maybe your partner is always the one planning date night. Take matters into your own hands, make all the arrangements, and surprise them with a night out on the town—playing, of course!

Choreplay

There is one gesture of pursuit that tends to go a long way when it comes to women, and that's pursuing her pleasure-center. In order for most women to relax into their pleasure-centers, they need to have a quiet mind.

You see, women carry an invisible workload. They're constantly assessing their home and family to ensure everything and everyone is taken care of. They're running lists of who needs new shoes or who has a doctor's appointment. They're tracking if they're running low on cereal, toilet paper, or paprika. They're planning for the kids' science fair, spirit week, lacrosse tryouts, and birthday parties. They're worried about the mean girl in her daughter's school and the baseball coach that's not giving her son a fair shot. They wonder if their home is inviting enough for guests and if they have enough allergy-friendly snacks on hand for the neighbor who's always coming over. They're pretty sure their husband is happy, but wonder if he's not telling her something. They balance the needs of pets, in-laws, neighbors, co-workers, teachers, and sometimes even the Amazon driver.

With a mind like that, is it any wonder that sitting down and relaxing long enough to "get into the mood" is difficult?

One of the most powerful gestures of pursuit a man can offer his woman is to lighten her load. This is counter-intuitive for an entrepreneur because early on, they agreed that he would focus on everything the business needs and she would focus on the family. If she accepts help in this area, it may feel like she isn't holding up her end of the bargain.

A big life takes a lot of hands, and sometimes this means you hire outside help to handle some of the tasks, thereby helping to lighten your partner's mental load. Sometimes, it means you pitch in at home more with lightening the workload. This can be as easy as a quick scan of the house to see what needs to be done. Dishes in the sink? Wash 'em. Basket of clean laundry sitting on the table? Put it away. Loose drawer always falling off its track? Fix it.

This is called choreplay because just like foreplay can help loosen a woman up, so can lightening her workload.

Divorce is Not an Option

Another common barrier to pursuit is a mantra that I hear proclaimed proudly, but without examination, that may cause more harm than good. That mantra is "Divorce is not an option."

While this seems like an honorable declaration, it may be keeping you out of the pursuit game altogether. Let me explain.

When you treat your marriage as if divorce is not an option, does it create a space for low standards of care to exist for too long?

Does it allow you to rest on your laurels with the understanding that no matter what, you'll stay together? If you believe divorce is not an option, has this created an iron-clad permission slip to become lazy in your marriage?

What if instead, you treated your marriage as if divorce is *always* an option? That notion forces you to consistently show up like you did in your courting days, with your best foot forward and learning the evolving needs of how your partner needs to be loved. This awakens your hunting skills and puts you on the prowl for who your partner has evolved into, and who she'll become next.

You see, marriage, when you're paying attention and doing it well, allows you to be with dozens of women over the course of your union. I'm not talking about dozens of different women, of course. I'm talking about dozens of iterations of your partner. Continually hunting her down and working to impress her ever-evolving nature will help keep you in pursuit.

The Art of Pursuit

The ways in which we need to be loved evolve throughout our relationship. Communicating with your partner how your needs are evolving gives your partner a beneficial advantage in creating more intimacy in your relationship.

The Art of Pursuit isn't always about big trips or extravagant gifts. The Art of Pursuit comes down to The One Percenters. The One Percenters are the small but consistent gestures of thoughtfulness and desire you communicate to your partner.

These gestures are as simple as the following actions:

- plan a vacation that isn't attached to your business travel

- maintaining a hug for at least six seconds

- leaving her favorite coffee mug out for her each morning

- the sweet or flirty text during the day

- letting her catch you staring at her

- standing lunch dates with her

- letting her have the same interruptive priority as business does, which means you stop what you're doing to take her calls as frequently as you interrupt your time with her to take business calls

- having flowers delivered midweek when you're out of town all week

- meeting needs that aren't yours

If every few days you can find one small gesture that communicates your desire for your partner, you keep The Art of Pursuit alive in your marriage.

For additional resources on Pursuit, please click the QR code below for a free download to get even more clear about how to increase Pursuit in your relationship.

CONCLUSION

I know your relationship might feel hard at times. It might feel like there's just too much scar tissue and you feel like anything you say will get shot down. The thought of opening your heart and mind to the possibility of getting your marriage back on track may send a jolt straight to the pit of your stomach. You might feel paralyzed in fear and overwhelm, using every cell in your body to resist taking a wrecking ball to the entire relationship.

The tension of having to choose between growing your business and saving your marriage might feel like a lose-lose situation. You might feel like sinking yourself into your work is a much safer option than diving into your marriage with your spouse.

But what if, instead of the gnarly path of repeated cycles and going in and out of couples therapy, there was a fast and easy way of doing a pivot in your marriage?

What if there was a quick filter you could run your marriage through to see where you might need to recalibrate?

- Am I on the healthy side of The Alpha Spectrum?

- Am I allowing her to step fully into her Omega?

- Are we having fun together?

- Are we affirming one another more than criticizing?

- Are we going to the same place on the horizon?

- Am I contributing in more ways than just financially?

- Am I protecting her from threats both outside and inside the house?

- Am I frequently showing her I desire her?

A happy, healthy marriage requires two happy, healthy people. An extraordinary marriage requires two extraordinary people. As an entrepreneur, you have plenty of opportunities to identify and pursue your own version of extraordinary. Hold space for your partner to do the same.

Hold the vision of what's possible for you when you step fully into the empowered, Healthy Alpha that stewards you and your partner into an entirely elevated version of your relationship. See yourselves getting to a place where you no longer yearn for the early days of your relationship because the new reality is so much bigger than you ever could have imagined. Hold space for that, and allow your partner to expand on that vision with her own unique gifts and perspectives.

Create a marriage that has two sets of gifted hands, two sets of clear eyes, two sets of open ears, and two hearts that continually seek one another. Speak life into your spouse and give her an expanded vision to step into. Invite her, lead her, guide her, and most importantly, show her.

***

Thank you for taking this time with me. It truly is the privilege of a lifetime to be gifted with this mission. In the early days of my divorce, when the silence of an empty house and the loneliness of the dark of night hovered above my chest, I promised that that suffering would not be in vain. I vowed I would find a way to put all that suffering to use—and here we are. My personal journey and my professional experience have taught me so much, and finding an audience ready for transformation at this level is remarkably humbling.

Thank you for doing this work. I'm certain this will leave ripple effects for years to come. Keep going, and know you have a devoted fan in me, standing for your greatness and pulling for your marriage.

xo

Kelly

Kellyclements.com

YT: @kellyclements388

IG: @the_entreprenewer

ACKNOWLEDGEMENTS

Keira Brinton and Joan of Arc Publishing, for being a Holy Hell Yes from the beginning. You created a container of flow, creativity, and absolute magic every step of the way.

Rjon Robins, for naming this book in under two seconds. Elegance at its finest; thank you.

My guy, Joe, for your healthy encouragement. Your leadership allows me to relax into Omega—a welcomed change of pace for me. And, for sharing your daughter with me. Having Faith in the house adds an extra layer of accountability for being soft and strong.

My boys, Luke and Will. After all these years, you're still the reason I do this work. You're more than I ever could have dreamed of and more than I deserve. Doing life with you is the honor of an eternity.

** I have captured events and conversations from my memories and/or knowledge of them. In order to maintain others' anonymity, in some instances I have changed the names of individuals and places; I may have changed some identifying characteristics and details such as physical properties, circumstances, occupations, and places of residence.

** Although the author and publisher have made every effort to ensure that the information in this book was correct at press time, the author and publisher do not assume and hereby disclaim any liability to any party for any loss, damage, or disruption caused by errors or omissions, whether such errors or omissions result from negligence, accident, or any other cause.